The Bill Cook Story
II

The
BILL COOK
STORY
II

THE *RE*-VISIONARY

The last, lasting gifts of a regenerative genius

Bob Hammel

INDIANA UNIVERSITY PRESS

Bloomington & Indianapolis

This book is a publication of

INDIANA UNIVERSITY PRESS
Office of Scholarly Publishing
Herman B Wells Library 350
1320 East 10th Street
Bloomington, Indiana 47405 USA

iupress.indiana.edu

Manufactured in China

*Library of Congress
Cataloging-in-Publication Data*

Hammel, Bob.
 The Bill Cook Story II : the *re*-visionary /
Bob Hammel.
  pages cm
 Includes index.
 ISBN 978-0-253-01698-0 (cloth) —
 ISBN 978-0-253-01707-9 (ebook)
 1. Cook, Bill, 1931–2011. 2. Billionaires—
Middle West—Biography. 3. Businessmen—
Middle West—Biography. I. Title.
 HC102.5.C565H362 2015
 338.092—dc23
 [B]
                          2014036701

2 3 4 5   19 18 17 16 15

Unless otherwise noted, all images are courtesy Cook Medical or the Cook family.

Dedicated to

BILL AND GAYLE COOK

Richardson's Studio

Contents

Acknowledgments

From the start, this second phase of a Bill Cook biography was the idea of Bill's wife and long-time partner in business and philanthropy, Gayle. The Cooks' son, Carl, provided his own variety of assistances—particularly in bringing the charm of the Newport Hill Climb to the story—as did his wife, Marcy, whose contributions through her camera alone were invaluable.

So many more joined in selflessly along the way, many—by Cook Group preference—namelessly, forming a team that provided every kind of help needed: physical, in terms of manpower and expertise; practical, in steering the way from idea to publication; financial, an element in being able to provide the first two. And those don't even cover another indispensable area in simple encouragement and morale.

So many others came into the picture to play major roles: Dr. Larry Rink, whose knowledge of all dimensions of Bill Cook's struggle added years for more of Bill's accomplishments and enabled a better grasp for the rest of us of all that Bill overcame to keep achieving; Mike Walters, Kevin Meade, Mark Rothert, Chrissie Peterson, Tony Rolando, Carol Davis, Scott and Tracy Snowman, and Linda Woods in particular from Canton, Ill., where so many others also chipped in with special Bill Cook insights; Gunar Gruenke and the incomparable artists from Conrad Schmitt Studios, partners with the Cooks in so many marvels; Marsh Davis and Tina Connor at Indiana Landmarks, Larry and Mary Bemis at Newport, Jack Mahuron and Tracy Wells at Beck's Mill, and everywhere the incomparable Pritchetts: the late Richard as well as Charlie, Joe, Jon, and all. It took several villages, and they were all there—including, at the end, Carolyn Walters and Bob Sloan, plus Michelle Sybert, Pamela Rude, and the rest of the Indiana University Press family who ultimately and actually made this book happen.

They—and I—were all arm in arm with the truly countless number of other people from Bloomington, Canton, and beyond who felt comfortable in calling and considering themselves good friends of Bill Cook. That is one big fraternity.

Introduction

FOUR FRUITFUL, PHILANTHROPIC, FUTURISTIC YEARS

The basic Bill Cook story has been told—of the bright and bold (with just a touch of brash) young man who seemed headed for a career as a doctor in his pre-med days leading up to a Northwestern University degree. After military service and an introduction to life in business working for other people, at age 32, with great help from his wife Gayle, an Indiana University Phi Beta Kappa art major, he launched a medical-device manufacturing company with a $1,500 investment and built it to global, multibillion-dollar magnitude.

The biography *The Bill Cook Story: Ready, Fire, Aim!,* which came out in 2008, told of many other fascinating Bill Cook ventures and adventures, unveiled him as a near-peerless visionary, and introduced some unforgettable co-stars. For example, the Pritchett brothers, Richard and Charlie, who started a construction company on a shorter shoestring than Cook, once built Bill a little worktable at his request but wouldn't accept a penny back because "you can't afford us, Cook." They later lived a business wonder tale of their own as the virtually designated construction company for the constantly expanding colossus that Bill Cook built.

But it was Bill Cook's company and his many interests, including the philanthropy that his business success allowed him and Gayle to engage in, that were the crux of *Ready, Fire, Aim!*—the phrase came straight from the subject, Bill's personal motto that signified his eagerness to spend more time finding out whether an idea he had was good than in testing, testing, and delaying.

For me, the most pleasing aspect of writing the book was that William Alfred Cook, a man of so very many talents and interests, was around to participate in it, to contribute greatly and vitally to it, and to enjoy it—which I think he did.

His stories, his memories, his precepts, even his irritations were best self-described. Much would have been missing if only others had told *The Bill Cook Story,* if he hadn't been around to share the indescribable triumph of bringing back to life the 1900-era southern Indiana wonders—the spectacular hotels at French Lick and West Baden, if the story of his life hadn't been put together until he was no longer around to contribute to it.

I was driving to a dinner appointment in Indianapolis on Friday evening, April 15, 2011, when a cell-phone call from my wife informed me that Bill had died. Among the shock and the sadness, the flood of thoughts about so many people affected, so much one man had accomplished, so many dimensions of regret, I felt a deep gratitude to The Great Charter of all destinies that this one had worked out: *Thank God we did the book when we did it.*

The news that telephone call brought could hardly be termed unexpected, except it was. In the days and months immediately before his death, I was in the same building with Bill, saw him most days. Certainly I saw him aging, weakening, thinning. But I didn't see him dying. There's a finality to death that I guess I never really saw Bill allowing, so much a man in charge of everything always. Yes, there was that time he spoke of his heart problems, the hard but life-preserving workout program his trainer Kris Gebhard put him through, the diet adjustments:

> I don't fear death. I have no control over it other than what I'm doing now, to try to keep myself happy, content, working, not overdoing, not be too worried, do my exercises religiously, eat a reasonable diet—all these things I've tried to do because I don't particularly want to give it all up.
>
> Now, if I get killed, I'll sure as hell be mad.

He didn't get killed, and there was no indication at the end that he was the least bit mad.

The days that followed his death were unscripted but orderly, from announcement through Celebration of Life, six weeks in which the Cook company's global world operated in transition with a carry-on smoothness that surpassed the word seamless. A great man was mourned, and a great company kept doing its job. All was well covered, by newspaper and TV, locally and nationally, no doubt globally.

Still, what Gayle Cook called about two years later to suggest had never occurred to me: Would it be possible, she asked, to add a chapter or a portion to the book to make it a full-life biography, filling in the last four years of his life?

Gayle knew much better than I, but even on the outside looking in, I knew that by April 15, 2011, a lot had happened in those years since the last pages of *Ready, Fire, Aim!* were written in the summer of 2007. For Bill and Gayle Cook, those years were primarily philanthropic. The business of Cook Inc., the company's future and its present and—far more

Gayle Cook

than with most chief executives, who never understand as clearly as Bill Cook how much history shapes and influences key decisions—its past, always were in his mind. But he was comfortable in those final years to hear about day-to-day company matters from others whom he trusted to do things The Cook Way and to keep him informed of all he should know. Bill's son Carl, with whom he had daily conversations, was the prime representative of those "others."

So I went to work on an epilogue. That's what I conceived: maybe 50 to 70 pages summarizing the noteworthy work he had taken up in those years in his hometown of Canton, Ill., and a few other things he had done in scattered other places. Yes, Gayle, I thought, I think that can and should be done.

It took lots longer than I expected; *I* took lots longer than I expected. Maybe reaching my own upper 70s influenced that. But I like to think that a delaying factor, too, was that interesting new material kept coming up. The epilogue that would have meant republishing the 2007 book with a new back section grew into a book of its own. That meant inherent problems: for example, I couldn't assume that all readers would have read the first book and remembered every bit of it; references to people or things in *Ready, Fire, Aim!* at times would need explanation. But there also was a great, off-setting advantage to publishing a separate volume: there could be plenty of room for pictures and that would allow me to tell an invitingly visual story even better.

None of that compensated for the advantage that Bill's presence gave to preparation of the first book. How much better it would have been to hear what *did* move him to go to Canton, almost 60 years after he left it, to give a moribund town new life. How *did* he feel when he saw it bloom? Why *did* he . . . ?

The good thing is that he did live to see the town blooming—to be part of that, to hear and feel gratitude—and to do some other towering works of benefit to people and to culture.

There was a beauty, a perfection, even a charm to the timing of death: his last preservation battle just over, and won.

Such a good idea, Gayle. Consider this the converted epilogue's prologue.

The Bill Cook Story
II

PART ONE

Restorations

Beck's Mill, 1972.

One

Beck's Mill

2007

"Beck's Mill needs stabilizing. It needs to be
made operable again, because it is fed by a very large spring.
It would be wonderful to have a place like that
that kids could go to see."

—*Bill Cook*

*H*istory—at least its romantic version—records that young Alexander the Great wept in despair when his successes were such that he finally had no more worlds to conquer. In the realm of architectural rescue, Bill Cook never experienced such a moment. When triumph was at hand with the uniquely magnificent French Lick and West Baden hotel projects, he had a new target list in mind.

"After we get French Lick and West Baden a little more complete," he said in early 2007, "I think maybe I'll start getting more interested in Beck's Mill, which is out in the middle of nowhere, not too far from Salem. It would give me something to do. Beck's Mill needs stabilizing. It needs to be made operable again, because it is fed by a very large spring. It would be wonderful to have a place like that that kids could go to see, like the old one-room schoolhouses that are preserved. And it could be open during the day, to grind feed, like Spring Mill."

One of the world's most visionary minds was visualizing, and of course it happened.

DAM, PIPE, WHEEL, TURBINE—"INGENIOUS!"

For some time, a friend of Bill's in Salem, Jack Mahuron, had tried to interest him in restoring a really old treasure, the nineteenth-century grist mill outside of Salem in southeastern Indiana. Jack hadn't had to introduce Bill or Gayle Cook to Beck's Mill. Like the Col. Jones House of Indiana-Lincoln lore, it was a place the Cooks had found on their own in their early Bloomington years. When Cook Inc. was in its infancy, the company's two cofounders entertained themselves many a Sunday by taking young son Carl with them on auto trips that ultimately produced the booklet that came out in 1972 titled *A Guide to Southern Indiana*. The guide was popularly received, so it was updated and re-published frequently up through 1982.

"The cover picture of the very first *Guide* was of Beck's Mill," Gayle says.

This wasn't just a place picturesque and ancient. History seeped from every timber. Of course the Cooks were enchanted by the place, and not just for *A Guide to Southern Indiana*.

"This guide attempts to describe not only the traditional Southern Indiana attractions but also the lesser known points in between. There are many surprises awaiting the traveler who takes the side road and lingers in the villages along the way."

—William and Gayle Cook

No. 87—Beck's M

Cover of the first "A Guide to Southern Indiana," 1972. *Photo by Walt Niekamp.*

a guide to Southern Indiana

with Indiana Highway Map

Price $1.50

The mill was in Washington County, deep in southeastern Indiana, one county north of the Ohio River across from Louisville. Washington's county seat is Salem, a city two years older than its state. Its whole downtown is on the National Register of Historic Places, and so are several buildings. Its courthouse lawn has a memorial to its citizens killed in duty all the way back to the Revolutionary War. John Hay, Lincoln's private secretary and Secretary of State to Presidents William McKinley and Theodore Roosevelt, was from Salem. So was Everett Dean, Indiana University's first basketball All-American, first Big Ten title-winning coach, and as it says in Cook Hall, the iu basketball museum funded in large part by Bill and Gayle Cook, "The Father of iu Basketball." In Indiana, maybe only George Washington is tagged for greater paternity.

Salem was Indiana's one Civil War site of note. When John Hunt Morgan's raiders made the Confederates' lone entry into Indiana in 1863, his slice through Indiana included a brief takeover of Salem. At nine o'clock on the morning of July 10, Morgan's men took possession of the town and burned its large, brick railroad depot, all train cars on the track, and railroad bridges on both sides of the town. Morgan threatened to burn all the town's mills, extorting $500 before leaving six hours after arriving.

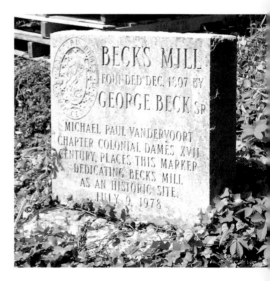

George Beck marker, at Beck's Mill.

A Beck's mill existed at the time, but not the present Beck's mill. It was built the next year, 1864, the third designed and constructed by George Beck on property he claimed after arrival from North Carolina in 1807, in Indiana Territory then, nine years before statehood. One day Beck noticed a waterfall from a cave on his property and immediately thought "mill!" It was special geography: the waterfall from a spring said to be Indiana's second-largest; the cave, a half-mile long, allowing water to flow even during the dead of winter; the site's elevation, 946 feet, among the highest in Indiana.

The land had been a Native American burial ground, in Shawnee and Delaware country. George Beck is believed to have been the first white man on that land. His first mill, 11 feet by 11 feet, stone and log, went up in 1808. A second, larger mill replaced it in 1825. The present mill, the first to have a second story, went up in 1864 and for the next 26 years ran 24 hours a day, a turbine/waterwheel combination turning its grindstones. Beck had built a small dam at a higher point west of the mill, creating the power source for all three mills.

"Ingenious!" Cook's architect George Ridgway raves. "For somebody to say, 'I'm going to dam up this cave, I'm going to put this pipe in, I'll run it over the top of the wheel, and then I'm going to take excess water and spin this turbine, which goes upstairs and turns the . . .' Two hundred years ago! The turbine we found out came from Philadelphia—that's where it was forged. So it had to come by barge down the Ohio, then probably up Blue River, then horse-and-wagon, or oxen."

By 1914, modernization had put Beck's third mill out of business. It was nearing a century of inactivity and minimal maintenance when things started to happen. One was the Cooks, with their *A Guide to Southern Indiana* passion. In the book, Gayle Cook had written: "There are many surprises awaiting the traveler who takes the side roads and lingers in the villages along the way. He should not be afraid to get lost. Some of our best discoveries were the result of unplanned meandering."

It's a lovely thought and perfect advice for the travelers' guide she and Bill put together, but it did not apply to their link-up with Beck's Mill.

"We had seen the mill, and we wanted it as a wrap-around for our first cover," Gayle said, "but the people we ran into would say, 'Oh, stay away from that. The man who owns that will chase you away.' We called ahead, told them what we wanted, and they said, 'Sure.' So that day we rushed down there with [Cook Inc. photographer] Walt Niekamp, and a guy was mowing the grass in anticipation of our coming. We got the picture.

"We went back to Beck's Mill a couple of times. We were exploring everywhere, and taking notes.

"Before that, we had gone to Parke County [which calls itself 'The Covered Bridge Capital of the World' for its 31 existing covered bridges] on the west side of the state. We had driven by the mills over there that were operating. Bill was fascinated by those mills, by the technology.

"This is the only mill that survived intact in southern Indiana. Spring Mill [an operating mill that is the centerpiece of Spring Mill State Park near Mitchell] was rebuilt. Everything was still in this mill. And the water source was still there. It was of interest just for being there."

Dam, supplying power to Beck's Mill.

Beck's Mill 2007, just before restoration.

A SECOND COMMA

George Ridgway came into the picture in 2007. "Bill told me when he and Gayle took those driving trips in the '70s, they came across Beck's Mill, which was in deplorable condition. It was owned by the Anderson family. Bill and Gayle wanted to invest in it then and repair the mill, and the Andersons said no. In the '90s they went through there again and made another overture, and were turned down again."

Then, Gayle says, picking up the story, "In recent years, 'Friends of Beck's Mill' was formed. Jack Mahuron, a retired businessman of Salem, shepherded it, kind of kept them on a businesslike approach."

Even Jack and his Friends "had not wanted any work done on the mill early on," Gayle Cook says. "Then they contacted us and said, 'I think we're ready to restore the mill now.' We said no—all our resources are tied up, the Pritchetts and everybody are at French Lick."

So, nothing happened. A few years went by, but when French Lick and West Baden were finished. . . .

At Bill Cook's request, George Ridgway lined up an opportunity for Bill, Carl Cook, and Ridgway to go inside the mill. "Of course it was in terrible shape," Ridgway says, "and Bill right away was telling me everything he wanted to do, just like he did with every other project: 'I want to fix this, fix that, take that wheel off . . .'

"I was standing there looking at the building, and Carl walked up: 'What are you looking at?'

"I said, 'I think I'm looking at a two-comma figure.' He said, 'Really?' I said, 'Yeah, I think I am.'

"He said, 'Let's try to do it for a high one-comma figure.'"

The key word was commas, as in setting off three-digit groupings within a cash figure—only one comma needed for anything up to $999,999. Carl was hoping to duck under $1,000,000, but Ridgway was on-target.

"When it was all said and done, we spent $1,215,000." A two-comma figure.

The night of their visit to the mill, Ridgway represented Bill at a "Friends of Beck's Mill" board meeting. He sat down, a stranger to all. "A guy from the New Albany office of Historic Landmarks of Indiana offered them a $50,000 matching grant," Ridgway recalls. "They had to come up with $25,000 and Landmarks would kick in $25,000, to do a feasibility study on fixing it up. They were starting to vote, and I said, 'Excuse me. Could I say something?'

Friends at work.

"I told them who I was and who I was representing, and I said, 'Now, before you commit to this money, here's another deal: Mr. Cook will pay for all architecture, all engineering, all construction—he will restore your mill, put it back in working condition, fix the parking lot, fix the grounds, and give the mill back to you. All he asks is the opportunity to do this for you.'"

The "Friends" were stunned, then explosive. "People had tears in their eyes, they were shouting at each other, all excited and upbeat," Ridgway says.

Ridgway had included one condition: "We have to be totally in charge." Experience had taught the Cooks that little proviso. "When we first started down at West Baden," Gayle recalls, "there were little committees forming, wanting to approve the paint colors and so on."

No such thing happened at Beck's Mill.

Work began in May, 2007. "We had to jack the building up, and lay foundation stone, which had to be laid historically correct," Ridgway said. The restoration was precise, helped by verifying evidence. "There were a lot of pictures of the mill, and all the original pieces were there." Wood two centuries old and rotten still told tales: "I know what size it is—it has to go from here to there," Ridgway said.

"When we opened it, we were using tooling that was 199 years old. We had to take it apart, repair as much as we could, and then rebuild pieces to make them function. And we made the old wooden loom work again. It was a neat project. It had been about ready to fall into that creek.

"It's all water-powered. There's a cave that goes back in the limestone country there about half a mile. They dammed up that water coming out of the cave and then took a round pipe that comes out of the cave pool and delivers water to the top of the overshoot—instead of water going underneath and spinning the wheel clockwise, it shoots over the top and spins the wheel counter-clockwise.

"I went back into the cave, probably about halfway, until the water got about chest-deep. I just wanted to see where the water came from. If you go up on top and know where the cave outlet is, you can walk about 50 feet away and see where it goes down a sinkhole and swirls. It's coming from a lot of different sources."

Creek, pipe-fed turbine wheel that was always Beck's Mill's power supply.

Bill Cook couldn't stay away during the construction. Pictures and videotapes taken during the work frequently show him right on top of things, sometimes hopping around in perilous places, scary to watch even knowing that nothing really happened to that spry man in his 70s, indulging his curiosities where no safety nets were around. Ridgway has seen those films several times and winces every time. "I think Bill had a lot of fun [walking on what amounted to narrow pipe]," Ridgway says. "He was up there looking over the dam to see how much water was coming through." It was perilous, Ridgway confirms. "I walked on it several times, and it was slick, it had moss on it, and it was wet." But he claims no responsibility for the film, or where Bill was when the camera was running. "I say, 'Now, Gayle, I wasn't there that day.'"

Walking precariously on slick pipes 15 feet above ground,
Bill Cook got his own good look at how a cave stream provided
the harnessed power for Beck's Mill. *Photos by Tracy Wells.*

After 11 months of work, the mill was operational in time for the 200th anniversary of the first Beck's Mill. The public opening was September 20, 2008.

As a follow-up in 2012, Gayle and Carl Cook "bought and donated the 79 acres around the mill, because Friends of Beck's Mill owned only the land that was right there, and the parking lot," Gayle said.

"One of the things I wanted to see before we bought all of that land was if they could keep it going with their volunteers. They have done a good job. They have an enthusiastic bunch of people—they dress up in their costumes. Seeing that they had a dedicated group and Jack Mahuron was still seeing them through properly on finances, we added that to it.

"They have trails in the 79 acres of woods around the mill now, and quarries and springs and cliffs, and a little cemetery. There's nice hiking around it."

George Ridgway says, "They use it as a museum, run it on weekends, charge admission, grind corn, and you can buy little memorial bags of corn flour."

It's a mill, functioning as it was meant to, all those years and all that technology ago. Borne out with every one of those little bags of corn flour is the guiding philosophy preservationist Bill Cook once gave for his way of selecting targets—saying yes to one restoration and no to another, the guiding principle: Can life be breathed back into the building? Can it live again as it was meant to live? He put it:

> I never like to do any kind of building and not have a prospect of making a profit. Just having a living history is not good enough. The building should be alive and doing its thing. You can't make every building a museum.

And Gayle Cook's concurring thoughts:

> Sometimes preservationists are not practical. They'll say, 'Oh, do *anything* to save the building.' But you have to find a use for it. That's a point we always make: finding a use is the key to saving architecture.

They certainly did operate as a team. In 2006 Gayle said, "We always say Bill likes the bricks and the mortar; I like the architecture, the history, and the interiors. So it works out." Bill called the two roles "the agony and the ecstasy" in a talk to students at the Ball State College of Architecture and Planning. Gayle's researching part, the fun, the ecstasy; his, the work, the agony. But

Sign above the entrance to restored Beck's Mill.

clearly there was a lot of enjoyment for both of them in the nearly 60 such projects they teamed to do.

Those projects also fit into another area that he described in a 2006 talk on "The Art of Giving" for the Bloomington Economic Development Corporation:

> We all have an obligation to society to give. If you are going to give, do so without the feeling that you are ever going to have a reward. One of the greatest kicks that I have is to see a gift come back in kind, where the gift means so much to someone ... it actually did some good to someone.
>
> Values come early in life. I learned from my father and mother. I learned from my classmates in high school and college ... from a lot of people over a long period of time. Gayle has had a similar upbringing. She also has that same idea that what you give, you get back manifold. She has been a great partner over the years. It's been a lot of fun being with the lady.

Two

Canton, Illinois

2008–

"And here comes Bill Cook,
not with hundreds of dollars—millions!
He gave us hope. He gave us life."

—*Michael Walters*

*E*ven the people closest to Bill Cook aren't sure how long he thought about it before he began the remarkable, even charming, resuscitation job he did on the hometown he loved: Canton, Illinois, which had been given up as moribund by most.

Harriett Beecher Stowe invented the best word for how that Bill Cook ruminating materialized into today's revitalized Canton. Like Stowe's twinkly-eyed slave girl Topsy's self-description in *Uncle Tom's Cabin,* every evidence is that it just growed.

And it's not done. As so many rusting relics that got their restorative TLC, particularly in the senior years of Bill and Gayle Cook, Canton today has an onward-and-upward look of its own momentum.

It's a kind of love story not new in Canton. It's hard to tell if it's more a case of man influencing town than town influencing man, but either way, "charming" still is what that love story is.

ANOTHER TIME, ANOTHER WILLIAM

Consider the Canton that William A. "Bill" Cook's parents rather chanced upon in 1940 when putting down roots during his childhood.

It's the same town that another man named William, a Massachusetts-born blacksmith named William Parlin, happened upon almost exactly 100 years before. Parlin apprenticed in his trade in his native Acton, Mass., and in his early 20s headed west: destination uncertain. "He simply stepped out into the unknown and began walking west as if he were looking for a prize," Michael Walters wrote in his 2013 book *Legacy: The Story of Three Families.*

The book is the story of Canton. Every town should have a Mike Walters. Mike is a Canton "lifer." He went through the schools there, worked in and then took over his dad's downtown NAPA auto parts store. A high school and Canton Community College pitcher good enough to get some letters of interest from the Cincinnati Reds ("that's as far as it went, just letters in a scrapbook"), Mike still coaches the high school baseball team; the 2014 season marked his 42nd year of involvement with the sport. And he has a passion for the town's history, his town's history, activated early when he lived

International Harvester's Canton plant. Right through
the Great Depression, an employment staple.

in a veritable museum. "My parents bought the Orendorff Mansion in 1970,"
he said. Living there "helped me get in touch with history. Finding out about
that house would lead to one thing, then another. I connected all the dots
with the Orendorffs, and all of a sudden here comes another family called the
Parlins, then the Ingersolls, the Hulits, the Underwoods, the McCalls . . . The
families just tie into one another."

At the center of everything are the three families of the book Mike and
Brooks Carver recently published: the Parlins, the Orendorffs and the
Ingersolls.

And William Parlin started it all.

Parlin's trek west from New England took him to St. Louis briefly, then he
swung back to Canton. He was 23 when he arrived in early summer 1840 with
"three hammers, a leather apron and 25 cents in his pocket," Walters' book
says. (The Cooks arrived in Canton in summertime 1940, in time for young
Billy to enter third grade that fall.)

In a city that had been incorporated just four years before, William Parlin
linked with a local blacksmith for a short time, then bought a foundry and in
1842 made Canton's first plow. It was a moment as providential as Detroit's
first car.

Parlin was meticulous about every part that went into his plows, personally selecting the timber used and approving every plow that went out. Throughout the 1840s he was in partnership with businessman Thompson Maple. That dissolved, but he needed someone to handle the business end and sales. By then Parlin had married Caroline Orendorff, and in 1852 he invited her brother, William, to handle those office roles for William Parlin and Company. By 1860, the firm had become Parlin & Orendorff Company, on its way to becoming by 1880 Parlin and Orendorff Plow Works, P&O for short: "the largest plow factory of its kind [with] the most complete and varied line of agricultural implements of any single factory on earth," Walters writes. Company literature of the time said: "We can equip a farm in any section of the known world with a suitable plow."

William Parlin

The secret: a plow blade Parlin conceived, developed, and patented that was angled at 38 degrees, which made it self-cleaning, new dirt pushing off the old. P&O's market even in those days of radically different communications and shipping quickly became worldwide. Its products by then included a double-plow, right- and left-bladed, fastened together so the soil was thrown on both sides of the furrow.

Parlin's plow became Canton's symbol—in truth, became Canton. The top of the line, the most famous plow in the world, was the Canton Clipper, "a household word with the Western farmers when the West ended on the banks of the Mississippi," company literature boasted, "invented and patented by William Parlin . . . perfect in shape . . . ran so steady that . . . any boy who was able to drive a team could use it . . . will be always a reminder of the past glories of the P&O Canton Line." In 1870, eighty employees in the downtown plant turned out 3,000 Clippers. By 1907, the plow works that Parlin began with personal, piece-by-piece involvement covered 18 acres; at its peak, it had 2,550 employees. "Most people living in Canton either had someone in their family or their next-door neighbor working 'down at the shop,'" Walters wrote. "The skill level of the city was enormously high. A patternmaker, an

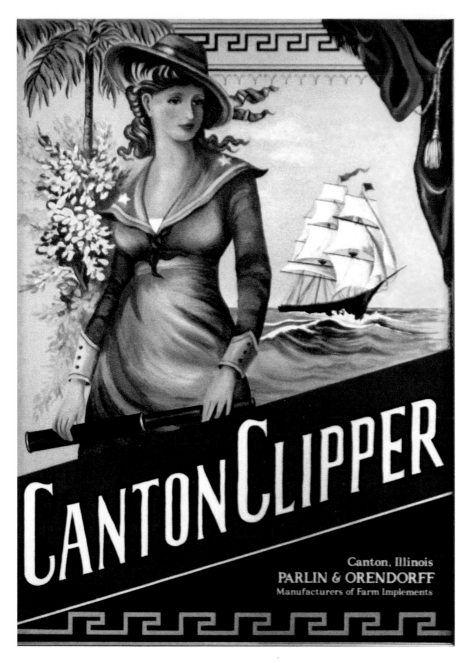

Canton Clipper. Internationally advertised and sold, the "P&O" plow that was Canton's symbol, the "top of the line," the most famous plow in the world. "A household word with Western farmers when the West ended on the banks of the Mississippi."

iron worker, a foundry man, a machinist, a draftsman, or some other highly skilled tradesman lived under nearly every roof."

The Canton High School athletic teams were called the Plowboys, and the basketball Plowboys reigned over the entire state of Illinois in 1928 as champions of the state tournament. Maybe that name was a bit rustic for someone; Canton teams are called the Little Giants now, but even the change was plow-related. It came in 1932, after International Harvester had bought the P&O Company, and "Little Giant" was the name of Harvester's top-of-the-line Canton-made plow.

In 1915, William Parlin joined reaper inventor Cyrus McCormick and meatpacker Philip Armour in the Illinois Farmers Hall of Fame, his portrait there carrying underneath the words: "What he did to feed the world is told whenever a farmer plows, a trader sells, a table is spread under the wonderful providence of God."

But the company's vast success was attributable as well to the "O" in P&O. William Parlin "could make a plow but he wasn't a very good salesman," Walters said. "So he took in his brother-in-law. One couldn't have done it without the other." Afterward, their sons—William H. Parlin ("a fanatic on quality control," Walters called him) and Ulysses Grant Orendorff ("dreamed of expansion")—carried on, "as with their fathers, a perfect mix. The company flourished."

William H. was the Parlins' only son who survived to adulthood. Ulysses—U. G.—was the fourth of six Orendorff siblings but the one who emerged as a company power, ultimately *the* company power. U. G. "did not have any hobbies, as other men did," Walters quotes Orendorff's 22-year secretary. "His hobby was making money and he was an expert at it." A Northwestern graduate, he rose from company treasurer to 50 percent ownership of P&O, and in the spring of 1919 at age 53, in a high-stakes business deal engagingly told in *Legacy,* he strode alone, carrying one business bag, into the executive board room of Chicago's biggest bank, sat down at a table of company executives and attorneys, and 4½ hours later walked out with an $18.5-million bank draft and attendant agreements that sold his 67-year-old family company.

Effective July 1, 1919, the P&O Plow Works, the huge downtown nerve center of Canton, was absorbed into the vast International Harvester line. For the next six decades, including Bill Cook's growing-up years, the bulk of prosperous Canton's economy rode, and rode quite well, on International Harvester paychecks.

ENTER THE INGERSOLLS

William Parlin's daughter, Alice, brought the third family name into Mike Walters' Canton triumvirate. An heir to her father's wealth and stock, she became Alice Ingersoll upon her marriage to Charles E. Ingersoll in 1880. Her husband "was a bed-ridden invalid for many years with a serious heart condition," Walters writes, and Alice's brother William Henry Parlin became a virtual surrogate father to her three children: sons William Parlin and Charles Dewey Ingersoll and daughter Winnifred. Both sons became officers in the company, and all three of Alice's children, like her, were major stockholders in the prosperous firm.

Ultimately, all three families—the Parlins, the Orendorffs, and the Ingersolls—contributed in many generous ways to the Canton in which Bill Cook grew up. The basketball arena where Bill played as a Little Giant was Alice Ingersoll Gymnasium, her gift to the basketball-loving community. Dedicated in 1930, it is still the Little Giants' handsome, 2,700-capacity basketball home, even though a new Canton High School was built and put into use several blocks away.

Ingersoll is the gym where young Bill Cook sank a shot that has a life all its own—desperation, end of the first half, of a length that keeps growing. Carl Cook remembers the day not long ago when he and his dad "were about 20 miles east of Bloomington in Brown County, sitting in a Nashville restaurant, and this older couple came up. The man said, 'Excuse me, are you Bill Cook?' Dad said yes, and he said, 'I grew up near Canton and I remember when you hit that full-court basketball shot.' He was five or six years old then, and he saw the game. It's amazing that somebody that young then remembered it."

The gymnasium is a living example of how all three family names still pop up on Canton businesses and buildings, but the true legacy from the William Parlin fortune, ultimately bequeathed through the estates of Alice Ingersoll's two sons, was a $70-million trust fund that in perpetuity blesses Canton as maybe no other similarly sized town is blessed. Dispersed annually through the community is almost 3.5 million dollars—a five percent annual interest return from the $70-million initial fund, which never shrinks.

Sample years listed in the Walters-Carver book record some $675,000 for the city's Parlin-Ingersoll Library; $445,000 for its Graham Hospital; $337,000 for Canton schools; $432,000 for city parks; $302,000 for Boy Scouts; $324,000 combined for YMCA and YWCA; $108,000 each to Red

Cross, Elks Crippled Children's Fund, and Salvation Army; $108,000 each to five specified churches: First Christian, First Methodist (the Cooks' home church), First Presbyterian, Wesleyan United Methodist, and First Baptist, and $43,000 each to three other churches: St. Peter's Episcopal, Trinity Lutheran, and Mount Carmel Baptist.

Every year, all those organizations and institutions can count on those gifts, which began with the Parlin plow. It's a novel, admirable form of benevolence, but obviously it had its limits as a sustainer for the community. Because Canton was a radically different city when the twenty-first century dawned, an ugly, uninhabitable cavity now where International Harvester-née-P&O had been. Even with the largesse of the community patriarchs, the town was dying.

THE LETTER

There is no mystery about when things began to happen involving Bill Cook and today's Canton. It can be traced to a letter sent to Bill on July 9, 2007, from Mark Rothert. A young man at the time heading up economic development in Canton, Rothert had read an interview with Cook in the Bloomington magazine, *Bloom.*

The interview was one of a very good magazine's finest moments: one of Bloomington's most noted achievers, Angelo Pizzo, the screenwriter of the movie *Hoosiers,* interviewing another, Bill Cook. Digested into a 4,000-word question-and-answer feature, one little segment of this wide-ranging interview particularly caught Rothert's attention:

> PIZZO: You've done a lot to revitalize the downtown area at a
> time when most cities Bloomington's size have downtowns that
> are dying.

> COOK: Conceptually it works very well. I wish it could have a little
> more retail, but it is growing. But we do have some problems in this
> town, things we have to guard against.

Rothert grew up in the post-International Harvester Canton. "My dad worked with IH. They transferred him out. I grew up in the '80s with all the depression that had hit Canton—never really benefited from the boom. I graduated from high school in 1997. I had always heard the name Bill Cook—how successful he was, and he was from Canton. In the article in *Bloom* he talked about historic preservation, and—him coming from Canton—I

Above. Canton's symbol: the most productive plow works in the world. *Postcard, vintage 1930s.*

Left. Canton's ugly downtown scar after International Harvester's pull-out and the subsequent fire.

really felt a strong connection. Part of my job was downtown revitalization. I wanted to go to the expert—to reach out, to pick his brain, because he talked about doing all those things in Bloomington and that's what we wanted: to do those things in Canton. Harvester was gone, the buildings were demolished, we had this huge 'brownfield' [an environmentally contaminated] site in the middle of our community, dilapidated buildings, a lot of vacancies in our downtown. We were looking for strategies on ways to change that."

And that's why Rothert typed out a note:

JULY 9, 2007

Dear Mr. Cook:

My name is Mark Rothert and although we have never met we
share a common bond of growing up in Canton, Illinois. I read an article about you in the Dec./Jan. 2007 issue of "Bloom Magazine" and
thought I would write. Canton has probably changed since you grew
up here, but it was a great community then and still is today with much
potential. However, Canton does face some major challenges. They include the former International Harvester brownfield site, deteriorating
housing, fewer employment opportunities, and a declining downtown.

I am the director of the Spoon River Partnership for Economic
Development, a local 501(c)(3) charitable non-profit economic development organization for the Canton area, tasked with bringing
new development, jobs, investment and business to the area, including revitalizing the downtown and the former IH site. I understand
you played an integral role in the revitalization of Bloomington's
downtown. I would be interested to come to Bloomington and
meet with you to learn more about your past projects, talk about
what we hope to achieve in Canton, and gauge your interest to help.

Basketball and music aside, I know you also deeply care about
community, preservation, and producing results out of ideas. Your
philanthropy in the Bloomington area to provide for the community,
preserve historical sites and create results is truly admirable. It reminds
me of what the Orendorffs and Ingersolls did in Canton so many years
ago. Canton was once a booming town but has taken many hits over
the past 30 years as I am sure you are aware. However with the support
of successful Canton natives, we can become as proud of our city's
future as we are of its past.

Thank you for your time and consideration of my request.

Mark Rothert
EXECUTIVE DIRECTOR
Spoon River Partnership for
Economic Development
City of Canton, Illinois

Less than two weeks later, a response came:

JULY 20, 2007

Dear Mark:

Thank you for your letter. As you know, Canton has always been a special place to me.

You are more than welcome to visit Bloomington and discuss the problems I see in Canton. We can tour Bloomington and have a look at what has happened in the last 25 years to this city. Mrs. Aimee Hawkins-Mungle has my itinerary and she can set up a day we can be together.

Best regards,

William A. Cook
CHIEF EXECUTIVE OFFICER
Cook Group Incorporated

"We set up a date with Aimee, and that started the ball rolling," Rothert said. "We" included Kevin Meade, at the time a city alderman but ultimately the mayor who in the view of many, including Gayle Cook, was the key in the ultimate tight link-up between Bill Cook and the town he considered home. "Kevin was my board president," Rothert said, explaining his presence as the second traveler to Bloomington.

The trip scheduled, Rothert and Meade prepared themselves as best they could. Charlotte Van Sickle, whose husband Jim was with Bill in the group of 1949 Canton High graduates who maintained a remarkably tight lifetime relationship, was Kevin Meade's neighbor. Meade remembers the conversation he had with Charlotte the day of his appointment with Cook:

KM: We're getting ready to go meet Mr. Cook later today. Of course we've heard about him, but how do we start this conversation?

CVS: Well, Kevin, he's just a regular guy. Just talk to him like you would anybody else. I will just give you one piece of advice: Don't ask him for anything. Everybody he meets wants something. I'll guarantee if you do he'll say no.

KM: The purpose of our meeting isn't to ask him for anything, other than advice.

cvs: Oh, he'll give you plenty of that. If you're there more than half
an hour, he likes you. If it's just a business meeting, a half-hour, 45
minutes, you'll be out of there.

That last "half-hour, 45 minutes" part Meade particularly remembered, so
"when we met, and had lunch, and after lunch we took a ride, I thought: 'At
least we got past *that*.'"

During the ride, Meade recalls, "Bill suddenly says, 'Well, how are you
fixed for money?'

"I think Mark interpreted that to mean 'I might be willing to give some
money for. . . .' I thought he was saying, 'Am I going to be the only guy putting money up for this or do you guys have something going?' Mark started to
answer and I cut him off. I said, 'We're doing great. Dick Versace (at the time
the nationally known basketball coach at Bradley University in nearby Peoria) has just invested in a building downtown. Crawford's has just expanded
their business downtown.' I thought that's probably what he wanted to know:
that 'we're not here begging—if you'd like to be a partner, fine, but we're not
here for that reason, so to speak.'"

"Looking back on it," Rothert said, "I don't know if Bill ever had plans to
reconnect with Canton or not. Maybe he saw this letter as potentially an opportunity to reconnect."

The best likelihood seems to be that Cook saw the letter as the first indication that someone at Canton might listen to him after years of his steaming
over decisions being made that—negatively, he strongly felt—changed the
Canton he had grown up in, and loved.

"For a long time, he complained to his friends over there about what they
had done with the square," Gayle Cook said. "At one point they built a new
bank building and moved it into the square. Bill just thought that was the
worst thing they could do. And then they closed off the square so you couldn't
drive around it."

It's more of a jut than a close-off now. A car entering Canton from the north
moves up Main Street just fine and, in the very block that is the western border of the heart-of-downtown square, suddenly there's an interruption. The
curb and the berm and the sidewalk jut out at a 90-degree angle and force
a swerve, then another 90-degree swing back to resume the previous route
down Main on the other side of the jut.

Who, of Bill Cook's small-town upbringing doesn't remember cruisin'—
the nighttime ritual of teens packed in cars driving for hours around the same

loop, through the downtown, 'round the square, past a drive-in or teen spot, returning, always, to circle the town square? And a bank building had dared to violate that route!

Jim Murphy, who heads up the real estate wing of the Cook organization (CFC), had barely heard of Canton before repeated trips there during the Cook renovation years made him a virtual citizen, but he knew well what Bill was missing. "When that [bank] building was damaged by a tornado in 1975," Murphy recalled, "the city decided to build it out into the right-of-way, thinking they were going to close the square to pedestrian use only—a mall, prohibiting vehicular traffic. It was the wrong thing to do." Gayle also fully understood Bill's objection. "The square is just the center of things. I could never figure out why they did it. At the time there was a trend away from having cars downtown. It didn't work too well.

"For years Bill would tease the people at Canton about destroying their square." Then, in a separate building decision involving a shopping center on the square, "they built the Penney's store—the anchor for the square—facing *away* from the square.

"When those things were done is when he began complaining."

And, of course, Bill Cook's irritation involved a whole lot more than memories of cruisin'. A free flow to downtown traffic and commerce was the main casualty.

The bank's intrusion onto the square *was* the take-off point for the Cook-Meade-Rothert conversation at that first meeting in Bloomington, Meade says.

"I asked him, 'You've lived in Canton, you've come back a lot, you've obviously done things in downtown Bloomington, what would you recommend that we do to improve downtown Canton?'

"He said, 'Well, the first thing you do is move the god-damn bank off the god-damn square.'

"I said, 'Mr. Cook, the god-damn bank is now the god-damn City Building and we're not moving it, so what's next?'"

The words sound tense but the exchange was smiling. And what Meade said was an inconvenient truth. By then the bank was gone, but the building's new owner—the City—was there to stay.

Still, Meade had already passed a crucial test. Bill Cook was making his points to someone, and that someone was listening. Many years, many proj-

The first of Canton's Bill Cook Era celebrations. Ribbon-cutting on the completion of the Randolph Building project. From lower left: Mark Rothert, Joe Pritchett, Chris Cockerham, Donna Harbstreit (partially obscured), Nikki Johnson, Jim Murphy, Bill Cook, Carl Cook, Gayle Cook, Missy Towery, Mayor Kevin Meade, Dana Smith, architect George Ridgway, and Dennis Crawford. Rothert, Towery, Meade, Smith, and Crawford from Canton joined the Cook group in the cutting. *Canton* Daily Ledger *photo.*

ects, later, Gayle Cook said, "Possibly the key [to Bill's sudden eagerness to do something in Canton] was Kevin Meade, the mayor. Because he's a doer."

"IN THE MIND OF A GENIUS"

The first indication of Bill Cook's willingness came "at the very end of the conversation in his office that day," Meade said. "He sits back and says, 'I might be interested in doing something. Do you have any old building you need fixed up?'"

"Ooooh, we've got a lot of them. Take your pick."

"Well, which one would you think?"

"The Randolph Building, probably. It's large, it's on the corner, and it's for sale, too."

"How much do they want for it?"

"I don't have any idea. Mark, what do you think?"

Rothert: "Oh, $83,000 . . . $85,000."

"That's a fair price. Did you bring any paper work on it?"

"No, because we didn't come here for that reason."

"Well, get me something on it."

And the day ended. As private as it was, as few ripples as it made at the time, it's that day that now is etched in Canton history. The city's own website calls it "a meeting that would forever change the future of Canton, and provided a spark that would touch off a small Renaissance of development."

At the time, though, with none of that assured, Meade still was ebullient. On their drive back to Canton, he recalls, "I told Mark 'I'm convinced he's going to buy that building. But if we don't get anything out of this but this meeting, we have just spent three hours in the mind of a genius. How many people would give huge sums of money to be able to do that?'"

That meeting, though, "is what started it all," Meade says. "In November, Bill came to Canton to look at the Randolph Building. He wanted to see what condition the roof was in, and the building was in such bad shape there was no stairway to get him up there. We were using a lift to put up Christmas decorations on the square, and we used it to get Bill up high enough to see what he wanted to see. Our City Engineer [Keith Plavec] looked out the window, saw him on that lift, and said, 'What are you *doing*?' I said, 'Oh, Bill wants to take a look at the roof.'"

Carl Cook remembers: "I didn't go that time—he just went out there, spent a few hours, and came home. A few days later I was in his office and he said, 'they need an example of how to do a building correctly. I've decided we're going to buy the Randolph Building and redo it.'

"It surprised me at the time. I knew that town had been hurting for a very long time. That was a very slow death. Even in the '70s you had the sense that things weren't going to end well, even when Harvester was still a big employer."

Carl had his own fondness for Canton. "I always liked it there. It had a friendliness, a cohesiveness to it. When I was in middle school, we started going over there. The thing that struck me was how friendly the kids were. Being the son of a native helped." He remembered being out with a group of Canton teens. "The son of one of my Dad's friends was home from college, and when he would introduce me, he'd say, 'This is Bill's son, Class of '49,' and everybody knew who I was."

THE "Y" AND BILL COOK

On Feb. 19, 2008, Bill, Carl, architect George Ridgway and engineer Greg Blum flew from Bloomington to Canton. Ridgway says, "I had never been to Canton—just one day, he gave me a call: 'We're going to fly over to Canton and look at a building,'"

In the Randolph Building, they weren't looking at prime real estate, but they were looking at history. The tall building was the square's southeast cor-

Randolph Building, a downtown staple, *above,* before the restoration and *below,* after the restoration was complete.

ner anchor, built in 1883. "It had not been occupied for a long time," Ridgway remembers. "The roof on the back had fallen in. It was unsafe on the second floor—a direct shot all the way to the basement. I walked through the basement, trying to measure in the dark. After we started construction, we found there was a pit in the basement about eight feet deep and six feet in diameter, and I had walked right past it—I never even saw it." One misstep and . . . "That would have been *real* exciting. I'd have needed a snorkel."

Meade says, "After we drained it, you could see George's footprints. He was *really* close. No one knew the hole was there."

Carl well remembers the worn-out state of the building. "The old YMCA had backed up against it. You couldn't get to the upstairs. The stairs that led up to the second floor were in the section of the building that was torn down along with the old YMCA. One trip I did go up the ladder, to see the upstairs before anything happened. It was a mess."

Few things in Canton struck a sweeter note with Bill Cook than that old Canton YMCA, where as a boy he had once been so short of funds he was given a "scholarship." He went back to Canton in 1985 to speak at the Canton Family YMCA's 95th annual meeting, and he was back again March 5, 2010, at the 120th, a much more familiar figure in the community that time. His return talk included overhead display of some pictures from his Canton Y days in the 1940s, and he said, "You can see how much the Y is intertwined in my life."

That never ended. In Bloomington in the 1970s, chairing a committee looking at building the community a YMCA, he listened politely and then ignored a national Y recommendation that Bloomington forget the idea because Indiana University offered so many recreational facilities.

It wasn't the only such advice he dismissed before construction of what became one of the best-used Y's in Indiana. Bill Cook's longtime friend, lawyer, and confidant, Steve Ferguson, was also on that committee. He dryly recalls another night when building plans came in. "We looked at those plans and decided . . . they weren't appropriate. Bill did that dramatically, by throwing them in the wastebasket."

And, in his last months, Bill was in the forefront of site selection for a second Bloomington Y, which opened in fall 2013.

With that 2008 trip, the Bill Cook appetite for going to work in downtown Canton was whetted, the 125-year-old Randolph Building first up.

To Canton *Ledger* editor Linda Woods, that was the building that stood as a decayed symbol of a downtown in its last throes. "Every time I would drive by the Randolph Building I would think of its glory days. It had been so many years since it had been occupied. The side windows at the top had birds sitting in the space because the windows were gone. That is the heart of our downtown—one of our large, historic buildings. It was sad.

"All the downtown business owners thought somebody was going to sweep in—they were going to sell these rundown building to somebody who was going to pay them a million dollars, and they were going to get rich off the buildings that they owned and hadn't been kept up. When that didn't happen, the buildings continued to deteriorate, and that poor, beautiful Randolph Building sat there."

Bill Cook saw its pluses, its possibilities, Jim Murphy says. "It was relatively close to the old Y, and it was downtown. Bill liked to invest in downtown communities, knowing downtown was the heart of the community. Renovating that building took over a year. Then he started talking about the downtown."

Carl Cook remembers, "He said, 'You know what? I'm going to see if I can turn this downtown around the way we did Bloomington.' He knew he had to control enough real estate to do it."

After the Randolph Building, Canton's Cook-inspired new look came in a burst of separate activities. "Those acquisitions all moved very quickly," Murphy said. "He got interested in the shopping center downtown." A fire had burned that block; then it just sat there—the north side of the square. In 1973 some community members built the shopping center on the northeast corner of the square. The whole shopping center—with the anchoring JC Penney store facing away from the square—"was ugly, quite frankly," Murphy said. "And it had poor maintenance—*no* maintenance. So Bill said, 'We should buy that.' We did, but we couldn't change the Penney building's direction." He went ahead with the shopping center purchase because, Carl said, "He knew if he controlled that he could make the downtown.

"Then he heard about the Lewis Pharmacy, which was one of his favorite places growing up. He said, 'We'll do that one, too.'"

The pharmacy: that was the fun part for Bill Cook. It's a lot more than a drug store, and always has been. "It had been a pharmacy for almost 100 years," Murphy said, "a pharmacy and in Bill's day a soda fountain. Bill went there as a boy and bought a soda, or a milkshake." Ed Lewis Sr. bought the Gustine Pharmacy in 1937, and Ed Jr.—also a pharmacist—took over after him. His son Dave worked there as a boy but went into photography business, and after his father's retirement at 92, Dave ultimately sold the building.

No one is happier about the emporium's rebirth than the last of the Lewises to work there. "I still call it Ed's building," Dave says, smiling. "I pretty much grew up in that pharmacy. I'm really pleased that somebody has taken as much interest to keep something alive. Not a whole lot of people would have done that. Several people were interested in that building—two pretty serious. If people had started in there and failed, it would have been another setback. Now, I don't want to say it ensures the longevity, but the chances are a whole lot better."

Buying the place for restoration "was always tempting," Gayle Cook said, "because the interior was still there." So were the goodies of Bill's day or maybe a little before, retained in framed pictures that offered "Hot Fudge Sundae 20 cents," "Vanilla Shake 10 cents," "Strawberry Cone 5 cents," "Root Beer Float 15 cents"—prices now relics from a bygone era.

Etchings on a Sweet Shoppe table. BC, as in Bill Cook?

The capper came when CFC was able to talk Alice Herrick into moving her candy-making business a couple of doors up Main Street to expand the Lewis Pharmacy/soda fountain into "The Sweet Shoppe and Lewis Emporium." Bill Cook wasn't her first customer in the new location, but he was among the happiest. Not even in its heyday was the place that sweet.

"When we bought the Lewis Building," Murphy said, "it was on the list of the ten most endangered historic buildings in the state of Illinois. But even then it was in good shape. It had the chandeliers, and the marble floor—intact, in incredible condition. Bill remembered a particular soda-fountain marble counter top that was not there when we bought it. We found one and replaced what was there. But really we changed very little about the interior. Just cleaned it up." And added Alice Herrick's candy-making equipment.

Not in need of anything at all was the century-old rich mahogany paneling along both sides of the long room. The marble floor has the same era's six-inch checkerboard-style black and white squares. The place can seat about 30 and at lunch often does.

Today, the twelve-foot long, seven-row glass display cases, where once cigars were prominent, are loaded with Alice Herrick's chocolates, made right in the store in the area where Ed Lewis and the pharmacists before him would

One of Bill Cook's teenage haunts back in business.

select from rows and rows of the medicines that are preserved now in boxes in the basement of a nearby business building.

The soul of the place is the colorful nineteenth-century apothecary show globe, a football-shaped ceiling light which pre-dates even the Lewises. "That's part of the personality of the structure," Dave Lewis says. "I understand the original concept [with pharmacies] was you had a smaller one, in a front window facing the street, and that would alert travelers—if it was showing red, it signified you had scarlet fever in town; blue meant something else. That was the original purpose." The one handed down by the Lewises is green, an appropriate color in Canton these days.

Occasionally, the Canton of the prosperous 1940s-to-1960s reappears on the streets near "The Sweet Shoppe and Lewis Emporium." On September 10, 2013, on the hottest afternoon of that summer, the block of Main Street in front of the building was cleared, traffic barred, and the First Annual Sock Hop played to a happy mixed-age group. It went well enough that plans are to make it an annual event.

A HOTEL NAMED "HARVESTER"

The Lewis Building project was just part of a fast-moving, free-wheeling period that answered Bill Cook's dreams. And Kevin Meade's. "Bill and I were going back and forth with e-mails—Bill would say, 'I'd like to have . . .' something, and I'd say, 'I'm going to be over there on business tomorrow. I'll just bring it.' I wasn't, but I made a point to do it."

Things were happening on other fronts in Canton, not done by Bill Cook but because of what he had begun. "It was kind of like a rolling stone," said the man whose letter started it all, Mark Rothert. "You get one project started, and things start to steamroll ahead and compound on each other. In Canton, he started with the Randolph Building. People were just amazed by that, and then some took an interest in their own buildings. We were lucky enough to get some grant money from the state to help downtown store owners do some façade work. People just jumped at that. We were able to do twelve or thirteen buildings downtown—new façades, new brick work—separate from Cook, but all because of that one building."

Included in the post-Randolph Building flurry was something altogether new. "When we would go over to Canton, the Pritchetts and their construction people would say, 'Boy, was that motel awful,'" Gayle recalls. "The idea of having a decent hotel downtown came out of that."

Motels, unappealing ones, were all the town offered. Mike Walters says, "I remember years ago talking to Little League officials and saying, 'Can we get a tournament?' They said, 'No, you don't have a hotel.' And I said, 'We can't *get* a hotel until we have people coming in.' We were in a Catch-22."

No longer. Cook, through CFC, put up a brand new hotel, with the perfect-for-Canton memory-soothing name of the Canton Harvester Inn, on what Jim Murphy calls "the other corner [northwest] of the downtown," the last anchor building in the Cook approach that had worked so well in reviving Bloomington's downtown: strengthen the corners and the in-between business owners will do the rest. Clearly the handsome, compact four-story hotel met a need. Now a couple of years old, Murphy said, "It is doing quite well . . . exceeding our expectations. It's just beautiful—you just do not expect that nice a hotel in a small Midwestern town."

With the hotel on its way up, Murphy remembers, "Bill said, 'Now that we've done all this *work* downtown, we need to get people downtown to use these facilities and support these businesses.' When we restored a building, we wanted to put it to use." That meant attracting stores that would bring paying customers downtown.

About that time in Macomb, 30 miles west of Canton, businessman Dennis Moon was doing well with the Princess Shop for women. "In his travels through Canton," his daughter, Amanda Holland, said, "the Randolph Building sparked his interest." Bill Cook heard of the interest, so he and Gayle drove the five-plus hours from Bloomington, Indiana, to Macomb on their own check-out mission to see Moon's main store. He and Gayle walked in, late in the afternoon, near closing time, as strangers, and the only employee on duty at the time was Moon's wife, Kathy. She met Gayle Cook at the door with the message, "We'll be open tomorrow."

Amanda Holland picks up the story with a smile. "Gayle said, 'I just wanted to come in and show my husband.' She let them in. It wasn't until they sat down at the table that she knew who she was talking to. She was wide-eyed." All went smoothly from there, and Amanda Holland now runs the Moons' One East Boutique, the street-level showpiece of the Randolph Building and its first commercial tenant. "We're definitely in a great location—we're thrilled," Holland said. "Even when we first got here, you could tell people were excited. Now, with the addition of about fifteen businesses downtown, they're proud of the community again. People who live here invite their friends to spend the day here and go shopping. And I'm finding more and more people coming in from out of town. I had a woman in from Bloomington [Illinois, her hometown, a good 50 miles away]. A friend asked her to bring her over for a personal favor, so she had some time to spend in Canton. She ended up in our downtown square, and she was just delighted. She said, 'I will come back, just to come shopping.' From Bloomington! That's a compliment."

Dave Lewis's photography business, just up Main Street from his dad's place, is an example of older stores that saw hope and bought into the new push for a downtown face-lift. Till the Cook infusion, Lewis had used up all the

Dave Lewis Studios. "We followed on the heels of the Cooks' renovation."

optimism he had just keeping the place open in the 27 post-Harvester-closing years, when downtown businesses in Canton had no reason to see growth ahead, more likely a shriveling, of the town's economy, and its population.

Dave Lewis remembers mid-1900s Canton, then watching the downtown die in stages. "Harvester closed in '83. Then Caterpillar downsized. About the mid-'90s, reality really set in. A cumulative effect, kind of snuck up on you—when it hit, it hit big time. The banks used to be open Saturday till 3:00, closed Wednesday afternoon. Then they started closing at noon on Saturday. After that, you could shoot a cannon up Main Street and not hit anybody."

The Randolph renovation changed that. "People in my type of business are always concerned," Lewis said. "You have overhead, mortgages you have to be able to cover. I tried not to panic. You can work at it pretty bleakly or—you know your expenses, you figure out what you can do to cover everything.

"Then this [state-assisted façade] project came along, and that was a wonderful opportunity to do something with the front of my store. Once I got that done, I looked at the inside and thought, 'The wallpaper's been there 25 years, the carpet's old—let's just go ahead and redo the interior'—with *my* money. We've received nothing but positive comments." And positive actions. "On our side of the street," Lewis says, "all of our neighbors have done very, very nice things. We followed on the heels of the Cooks' renovation."

A MURAL OF OLD CANTON

Scott and Tracy Snowman operate an art studio in the same downtown area. "Every building that gets cleaned up puts pressure on the next person to clean up," Scott said. "We had seen what a snowball effect deterioration has. It happens the same way with positive change, too."

"All of a sudden Canton has growth," Carl Cook said. "They hadn't had growth for 40 or 50 years—four building permits issued in two mayor administrations, then in one year something like 17. Whatever it's related to, the fact is they're growing. They're getting stores."

Canton's new downtown still needed one last touch. That touch turned out to be Canton's old downtown.

As popular, as singular as any element of Bill and Gayle Cook's contributions is a four-stage mural that turned what Jim Murphy described as an "ugly blank wall" into a street-side Sistine Chapel ceiling. Canton-style. And vertical.

It's not small. Each of the panels is 16 feet wide and 12 feet high, side by side filling up a lot of a block. "Initially we just wanted to transform a big ugly blank wall [on the JC Penney building in the Fulton Mall, the side that does face the square] into an attraction," Jim Murphy said. To start, crews painted the wall a   -catching yellow. That wasn't enough.

In September 2009, Murphy says, "we commissioned the murals. I told Bill, 'It would be really great if we could find someone locally to do them.' Carol Davis, from Spoon River Community College, told me, 'I've got just the couple.'" That day Murphy met Davis's couple: Scott and Tracy Snowman, both artists, both Canton-raised and Spoon River-connected, both excited

The start of it all: Norris granary, purchased by George Cook, 1940.
Print, Snowman Studios.

from the first moment they heard of the possibility. "I shared with them our ideas, met with Bill and Gayle, and after about two months of refining that, we signed a contract," Murphy says. "We got the right two. They did beautiful work."

The scenes recreated in the murals are from early-1900s postcards of downtown Canton scenes; historian Mike Walters had a hand in delivering those, too. "We started with scales, doing what we could do with computers, sharpening them and enlarging them." Tracy said. "We would make a print, and hand-draw to get the clarity. Pen and ink. We generally work with a scale of one inch square means one foot on the wall."

Both Scott and Tracy are Canton High graduates. They left Canton, then returned in 1989—Scott as an art teacher at Canton High and Tracy at Spoon River College. Scott joined her in a faculty position there. Their return also marked their opening of a side-business: Snowman Studios, working out of their home. "The dream was always to have a store," Tracy says.

They already had gained a local reputation with a couple of downtown murals when the Cook opportunity came. "We had done several," Tracy said. Of course the artists were nervous on first meeting with Cook about the possible project. "You could not meet Bill Cook and not be intimidated," Tracy

Tracy and Scott Snowman.

said. Things moved fast from there. The paintings were done in about ten weeks. Showdown
time was when Jim Murphy brought Cook to the
Snowmans' house for his first look at the murals.
"They don't look big on a downtown wall," Tracy
recalls, "but they were just massive in our garage
space. We had to lay them flat, and you couldn't
see them unless you got up on a ladder. So we had
Mr. Cook get up on the ladder, and take a look.

"And we saw him so excited! Like a little kid!"

The murals are street scenes, each of the four
taking a familiar block of downtown Canton
back about 100 years. Two are the Randolph
Building and the Lewis Building, the original
buildings, pointing up how faithfully they have
been recreated. "The other two reflect what was
there at one time on that same street," Tracy
says. "We picked the pictures that we did because
somewhere in there is a building the Cook Group
now owns. The Randolph Building block was the
easiest to do, because that building still stands.
The others, we were able to use photographic reference, and that was very helpful. We'd stand at
the same spot where the old photo was taken in
about 1900, to get the perspective.

"It was a monumental amount of work. We
even had visions of Michelangelo and the whole
Sistine Chapel thing, how daunting that kind of
project is. And it *was* a daunting project. As we
rounded the corner on the fourth one, we felt a
little sadness thinking that it was coming to an
end . . . and a little pressure to put in anything
that we didn't get in the other three."

Each of the street scenes includes people, pictured on the postcards, re-
drawn for the mural, with live help. "Scott and our son Jake modeled for all
the men in the postcards," Tracy says. "I gave them beards and mustaches and
other things. And our daughter, Taylor, modeled for several of the women.

Looking northeast on Elm Street,
east side Canton Square circa 1900.
Mural by Snowman Studios.

Looking west on Chestnut Street, north side Canton Square. Behind the horse-drawn cart is Bill Cook, popcorn man. *Mural by Snowman Studios.*

Looking south on Main Street, south side Canton Square. *Mural by Snowman Studios.*

Looking east on Chestnut Street, north side Canton Square. *Mural by Snowman Studios.*

The fourth mural is the most personal for me. It's the only one I appear in."
On the street is a horse-drawn buggy. "Scott and I are in the buggy."

Each of the four murals, as a special touch reflecting their creativity and a
little bit of the Snowmans' taste for fun, includes a tiny, subtle, visible but eas-
ily unnoticed reference to the Cooks. It's there in one mural on a card inside a
window; in another, a little sign advertises COOK CANDY; the Cook name is in
the far corner of a third—"it's the most obvious, but it's the hardest for people
to find—so obvious they miss it," Tracy says. And the fourth: "That's where
we put Mr. Cook and a reference to Gayle as well." Clue: find a popcorn
wagon, and note the distinctive name "Gayle" spelled out on it, with a little
heart as well. And the popcorn man is drawn as Bill.

Once drab, now a landmark.
Site of the murals on Chestnut Street,
in front of Fulton Square.

Inspiration for all of that "really came from Mr. Cook," Tracy said, "because he sent us to French Lick to see what already had been done. Before we went, Jim Murphy said, 'Hey, be sure you find Mr. and Mrs. Cook in there because they're hidden in those murals.'"

Bill Cook always insisted the talk that he was in a French Lick mural was myth. Murphy says otherwise. "Walk in the main door at French Lick, take an immediate right, before you go out into the next room, the hallway, look up—the mural on the right-hand side. You can tell it's Bill and Gayle."

"That is so cool . . . brilliant!" Tracy Snowman said. "We just loved that. We thought, 'We've got to find a way to sneak that in here.' We ended up getting the Cook name in each mural. That meant a lot to us."

Historic Downtown Canton marker,
with water tower. *Painting by Snowman Studios.*

Canton Mayor Kevin Meade and Bill Cook at
downtown murals dedication.

The days that live forever for Scott and Tracy Snowman are those when the
murals were installed, then unveiled, and finally dedicated.

The climax was a festival on Friday, September 24, 2010, a community ice
cream social at nearby Jones Park, a full-scale ribbon-cutting in front of the
murals, Bill Cook, Gayle Cook, and Mayor Meade all joining in for official
dedication of the murals. "That was the most exciting day of our career, hands
down," Tracy says.

"But the most thrilling was the day they were installed."

That was a month earlier. One by one the murals went up, in one Au-
gust day. Downtown Canton wasn't a very safe place to be driving that day
when the citizenry, unaware any such thing was planned, suddenly saw the
new artistic landmark taking shape. "It was one big traffic jam," Tracy says.
"We sat on the square in our car for more than two hours and just observed.

Preserved postcards were the basis for murals. East side, Canton Square.

Jones Park, for decades the hub of Canton's Downtown Square. *From postcard.*

People were swerving, stopping their cars—not only stopping: getting out and *screaming*, and talking! Just fascinated."

The wall and street run east-west. "But even if people were going north-south, they could see them, and they would change directions and here they'd come," Tracy said. "I've never seen anything like that in Canton. I don't think up to that point we even would have dared to use the word masterpiece. But as we saw them installed . . ."

A THURSDAY AT A CHURCH

For all the business changes, all the prettying, and the step-up in sales, no one questions the biggest day of all in Canton's rebirth: December 11, 2008. A Thursday. The day the whole town seemed to gather inside jam-packed First Baptist Church.

Until then, there still was that downtown hole. That blight. That monstrous property right downtown that once represented the city's beating heart, the P&O Plow Works, then the International Harvester plant, but now was an ugly, gloomy lot, contaminated with the governmental tag of brownfield.

By federal definition, a brownfield site is ground that once was in use, most commonly as an industrial site, but now is vacant and dubious for immediate reuse because of the likely "presence or potential presence of a hazardous substance, pollutant, or contaminant." It can be sold, but that brownfield designation is the ultimate caveat emptor, "let the buyer beware," and it kept the abandoned International Harvester site unsold and unsellable for more than 20 years. It was the town's Grinch that wouldn't go away, a 30-acre mockery, a reminder that once that very site was the reason the whole city felt lucky and prosperous and invulnerable to economic ups and downs because, since way back in the 1800s when William Parlin came up with that plow and P&O made the world its sales market, Canton always had jobs, and jobs meant money.

Anthony V. "Tony" Rolando is the Illinois Department of Commerce and Economic Opportunity's region representative. Though not a Canton native he's local enough to know the town's recent history and what that brownfield meant. "I'm from Farmington—came to Canton in 1975, had a store on the south side of the square, 25 years in that business. My dad worked in the coal mines around here."

A twenty-first-century visitor to Canton doesn't sense a coal-mining atmosphere.

"Oh, yeah, all around here—this was coal-mining country. In the 1930s they started strip mining. There was a mine up in Norris [the crossroads town north of Canton which had the granary that George Cook bought to bring young Bill Cook to Canton], there was a mine at Little Sister—every little town around us had a coal mine. High-sulfur mines—they mined it and burned it right here. Then EPA laws changed. It was just not profitable.

"My dad lost his job in the '80s. But nobody here really paid much attention. There were only 200 coal miners up there. Then Hiram Walker closed, and Pabst Blue Ribbon brewery closed—Peoria was a distillery-brewery area and a lot of Canton people worked over there. Then in Peoria Caterpillar cut back its work force tremendously, and a lot of our people worked there." But in Canton, Harvester hummed. Or seemed to.

Over the years, a century-plus of years, Tony Rolando says, smug Canton "turned away a lot of business—this company wanted to come, that company wanted to come, back in the heyday. 'We don't *need* anything else. We've got International Harvester. They'll always be here.'

"But by the '80s International Harvester was already cutting back. In the late '70s, a couple of thousand people worked there. Then it was down to about a thousand, and they just kept cutting back till it was closed."

And one day—that 1983 day when International Harvester finally and totally left—Canton woke up to a sad new world. That day was Christmas Eve, Meade says. "The gift to Canton that Christmas was doubt and uncertainty."

"We lost . . . a lot," Tony Rolando said. "The demeanor of the people got bad. Negative. Hopeless. Pessimistic. 'Canton's dead.'

"This town was made up of a lot of strong, old families, a lot of Croatian families, hard-working folks of all nationalities—they just left. It was 'turn the lights off when you leave town.'

"We lost self-respect. We lost our families. We lost our soul."

Unemployment neared 20 percent. "It was," Tony Rolando said, "just as bad a time to be here as could be." Meade kept a Winston Churchill quote on his desk: "When you're going through Hell, keep going."

Then, in 1997, Canton's awful situation got worse. The abandoned Harvester factory burned in a spectacular fierce, raging fire. "We stood and watched," editor Linda Woods said. "I saw the last of the building—the big tower—coming down. One fellow wandered in from right there in the neighborhood and said, 'They'll never do anything with that site.' I wanted to tell him: '*You've* lost all hope. The rest of us haven't.'

"It wasn't vandalism. They did find arson, and they did make an arrest. The joke around town was that the gentleman who started the fire did us a favor."

But not much of one. After the fire, Rolando said, "The site was just, literally, a brown field. The whole block had been razed, there was nothing there—a lot of hope and not much promise." Surely the place would have an attraction to someone, Canton people kept thinking—available real estate, right downtown, once so very valuable. "A fellow looked at putting a movie theater on the site," Rolando remembers. That nibble prompted Meade to put together his "brain trust"—City Attorney Chrissie Peterson, Mark Rothert, Rolando, and Carol Davis, representing Spoon River Community College. The deal fell through.

So did another aimed at putting a restaurant there.

Scott Snowman recalls hearing that Pella Windows was looking for a manufacturing spot. It kept looking. So did a company that Peterson said looked at putting up a call center to help people get back in line with their student loans.

"All of those were very public starts and stops," Chrissie Peterson said. And build-ups and letdowns for close-watching Canton.

"We tried desperately to get a state prison in the '80s," Tony Rolando said. "We had been turned down on that. Then we were successful. I guess it was a success—it *was* a place for people to work."

"There were a few rays of light," Meade said, "but the fire let us know we had to start over."

A SIXTH FACTOR

The site's ugliness—"just a giant wasteland," in Carl Cook's term—was omnipresent for the First Baptist Church, one of those five primary beneficiaries of the Ingersolls' bequest. First Baptist was located straight across the street from the brownfield, the church's front door sending worshipers out its main entrance every Sunday morning face-on into that view. The church's pastor at the time, the Rev. Keith Jones, told Linda Woods for a *Ledger* story, "One day we walked along Elm Street there and decided to do something to beautify this site in hopes of bringing jobs and lifting the spirits of Canton residents." He organized a prayer vigil and, Woods' story said, got prayerful help from fellow Canton ministers Kenny Bloyd, United Church of Christ; Michael

Brooks, St. Peter's Episcopal Church; Kevin Kessler, Church of the Brethren; Maureen Stein, Trinity Lutheran Church, and Kevin Van Tine, Covenant Community Fellowship.

And just about that exact time, miles away in Bloomington, Indiana, Bill Cook moved his thoughts from reviving downtown Canton to revivifying its industrial heart.

Necessity played a part. The Cook company's long-established preference for self-supplying when possible rather than paying a middle man came into play. "For years we talked about building some kind of satellite plant where we could just move some commodity stuff that might have unique technology so we don't have to completely outsource it," Carl Cook said. "Not something where we needed a lot of engineering or research—where we could just make it ourselves. We had been looking at Florida, small towns—people were batting around all sorts of places.

"Finally, Dad said, 'We're going to put it in Canton.'"

How he said it was classic Bill Cook.

A fundamental part of George Ridgway's job as the Cook company's primary architect is advising on dollars and sense in building. "Bill had already told me he wanted to build it in Canton," Ridgway recalls. Still, the architect ran his studies and took his findings with him into a one-on-one meeting with Cook.

"I said, 'Bill, I've got five reasons why this building should be built in Bloomington, not Canton. Here are the five.' I got to the end and he said:

"OK, George, are you done? Is that your five?"

"Yes."

"You forgot a sixth reason: I want it in Canton."

So, Carl says, "from the very beginning, he gave the order: 'It's going there. Whether anybody else likes it or not, the plant is going there.' Later on [when a second plant was added on the site], that was Canton-guaranteed also, 'It's going there. I know it makes sense to put it some other place, but it's going there.'"

But no one in pessimism-prone Canton knew that. And even within the Cook company it wasn't an altogether done deal. There still were barriers to clear. There still was that brownfield, with its development-inhibiting laws. Bill Cook wasn't about to blink.

Things started to go public on a Tuesday at "about seven in the morning," Kevin Meade recalls. "I was still in bed." The phone rang. "The first thing Bill said was, 'Tell me about IH.'"

"What do you want to know?"

"'Do you have the paperwork on it? The environmental stuff on it . . . that kind of thing?'"

Meade wakes quickly. "I said, 'Bill, I'm going to be in Bloomington tomorrow morning. Why don't I bring all that stuff over to you?'

"I wasn't, of course, but I was now."

Chrissie Peterson's phone was the next to ring. "Kevin asked me to 'put together some stuff about the IH site.'

"I said, 'What kind of stuff—environmental report, legal description . . . ?'

"'I don't know, just find me some stuff that might be important.'

"So I printed off the environmental report, and I thought, 'What's in that report is going to kill whatever positive outlook the man has.'

"Mr. Cook had inquired about the northwest corner of the site. That portion is the dirtiest, where the really heavy foundry work occurred. We have some levels of arsenic, compounds—all the things that send the EPA up in arms.

"The northeastern corner of the property was relatively clean—about five acres (of the plat's thirty). We sent him information about the northeast corner and the northwest corner. We thought if they're going to build anything of substantial size they're probably going to need more than five acres." The Cook purchase ultimately covered seven acres, the company doing its own clean-up while promised payment from the IH end was awaited. And still is.

Meade showed up as promised at Cook's office the next morning and—surprise!

"I thought it was just going to be me meeting with Bill, but I walked in and there's Jim Murphy, [Chief Operating Officer] Scott Eells, George Ridgway . . . Connie Jackson was there to talk about Human Resources, John Kamstra to talk about finances—five or six people, most of which I hadn't met. I didn't know I was doing a presentation, but as I talked it was obvious that they knew a lot about what I was showing them. They had done their homework."

It was a clue things were farther along than Meade knew, but Bill Cook still wasn't tipping his hand.

"Bill said, 'We're going to build a plant. We want to look at that site,'" Meade recalls. "That was on a Wednesday, and the following Tuesday they flew in to Canton." They looked and went home. Wednesday, then Thursday passed.

October 3, 2008, a routine Friday, although a bit of a testy one, shaped up in City Hall. "We had a liquor commission hearing scheduled that day, with a

The downtown site that was the manufacturing hub of Canton for more than 100 years and an eyesore for about 25 is green and booming again, thanks to Bill Cook's decision to locate first one, then a second manufacturing plant in the town where he grew up. The first to go up, in corporate terms "Cook Canton," manufactures catheters, and the second, "Cook Polymer Technology Canton," is nicknamed PTFE for the polymer tubing produced there. Together, their employment is nearing 200 people and rising.

local liquor license holder who just wouldn't comply with the rules," Peterson said. The obstinate license holder was running straight into trouble. "We'd had long meetings about how this hearing was going to go and what the punishment was going to be."

Just before the hearing began, "exactly at two o'clock, they're walking in my office for the meeting and the phone rings," Meade remembers. "I said, 'I've got to take this call,' and excused myself." This call was The Call, from Bill Cook.

Minutes later Meade rejoined the group, and the get-tough script had changed, Peterson said, "Whatever that liquor license holder proposed, Kevin said, 'That sounds great! Let's do that! Yes, we can make that happen! That's not a problem! I *know* we're going to get things together!'

"My mouth was hanging. I'm thinking, 'He agreed we're going to do X, Y, and Z, and now *this*?' And I think, "The mayor's in a really good mood today." And then he disappeared.

"About an hour later, he summoned us all to his office—and now I'm thinking, 'At four o'clock, on a Friday afternoon . . . this isn't going to be good news.'"

"AND, BY THE WAY—69 DAYS"

The summoned group was the brain trust—Peterson, Rothert, Rolando, and Davis. "When we all got there, he had a big grin on his face," Chrissie Peterson said. "He didn't say anything. He reached under his desk and pulled out a bottle of champagne—'Cook' label champagne.

"And he said: *'He's going to build it!*

"'*Bill* called. He's going to build a *factory*—45,000 square feet, employ up to 300 people. . . .'"

"We were in tears," Rolando said. "All of us had lived through that whole time. The thought of actually having a factory on that site was just unimaginable."

Peterson recalls: "Kevin let the celebration go on, the champagne flow, and the tears, too, for about an hour, and then he tells us: 'And, by the way, we need to have this project ready for an announcement by December 11, 2008.'"

Just 69 days away. Less than ten weeks.

"We've had a couple of glasses of champagne now so everybody went, 'OK! Sure!'" Peterson said.

"Sometime over the weekend, the reality of that date set in. Monday morning, the City Engineer [Keith Plavec] and I were waiting in his office when the mayor came in.

"I ticked off a full list of things that had to be accomplished: 'We have to go through the statutory process of selling the land. We have to get a prospective purchaser agreement through the EPA. We have to get an environmental insurance policy with AIG (the insurance company that holds the environmental insurance policy on the site). We have to vacate the old plats, re-subdivide the land, not to mention we have to deal with [IH successor] Navistar and our current settlement agreement because our original agreement covered only five acres and now we're talking about something bigger and there's money in an escrow account that has to be dealt with.'

Kevin Meade

"And then the City Engineer starts in: 'I need to build a new road. I need a water line. I need a sewer line. I probably need to bury some power. I'm not sure that the gas extension is going to be able to deal with storm water drainage. And, oh, by the way, we've got to remove all the concrete that's already sitting there and get the EPA to bless all of this . . .'

"And the mayor just said, 'Okay.'

"We're looking at him thinking we've just rattled off problems that are going to take two years, and millions of dollars, and this is his response? 'Okay?'

"Keith and I looked at each other and thought, 'Did he finish off the champagne this morning?'

"And then Kevin said: 'At the groundbreaking, should we have gold shovels or silver shovels?'"

"For a couple of seconds, we just stared at each other," Chrissie Peterson remembers.

Then Kevin Meade did more than answer, more than explain. Turning quite direct, he told his chief aides:

"You two haven't told me anything yet that kills this project.

"Chrissie, you've got some timing issues, and Keith, you've got some money issues and some bid issues. But you haven't told me *anything* that kills this project.

"From here on out, I only need one thing from you guys. The answer has to be 'Yes!'

"No matter what the obstacle, this project is so important to this community, our answer has to be 'Yes!'

"Whatever the problem is, find a way around it, over it, through it."

It's a favorite, treasured memory of Peterson, who says with a smile: "We reminded him of this later when the city was getting new cell phones. Someone from Cook told us they were getting 3G capability and we said, 'OK, not a problem!' Then we had to Google it later because we had no idea what 3G was." (In cell-phone talk, it meant third-generation—a gauge of advancement and development that's reached 4G now, on its way up.)

"It was," Peterson says, "a very busy 69 days."

Kevin Meade just smiles. "It really was an amazing ride, those next 69 days."

KEEPING A BIG, BIG SECRET

Meade demanded one more beyond-all-human-instincts thing from his cohorts: silence. Heart and mind racing from knowing the town's biggest news in years, they were ordered not to talk about it.

"We weren't telling anybody," Meade said. "Even the aldermen—I called them in one by one and told them, 'I'm going to have to ask you to vote for stuff, but you're not going to know what it is. Just trust me, it's going to be good.'

"I'm a fairly new mayor at the time; I've got a couple of aldermen who are very independent. They wanted to know. I said it couldn't get out. All of the aldermen but one agreed. I told him, 'You can do what you want.'" One protest vote wouldn't stop anything, Meade reasoned. Talking might.

"We kept that thing so quiet," Mark Rothert says. "About five or six of us. It was unprecedented. But we knew the importance."

"To qualify for one of the grants, we had to show that we had matching funds," Chrissie Peterson said. "At that point, no money had been budgeted, so we had to go to our local hometown bank and say, 'We need you to write us a letter of credit for $1.9 million and we can't tell you why.' And they did it. Some of the aldermen weren't aware of the full scope of the project until the day it was announced."

Aldermen were one thing. The media were another. To a reporter, nothing beats the thrill and pleasure of breaking a news story that becomes the talk of the town. And nothing beats the agony of "sitting on" a news announcement—knowing about it but temporarily holding back, for any number of reasons, most commonly involving news heard in confidence from a consistent and important news source—and seeing it come out first in a rival publication or media source.

In Canton, Illinois, stories don't get any bigger than

BILLIONAIRE BILL COOK TO BUILD FACTORY ON IH SITE

But, somehow, Kevin Meade kept that bombshell bottled up.

"I didn't know it that far ahead," Canton newspaper editor Linda Woods said. "We were made aware there was going to be a big announcement. I think we had a small 'head's up.'"

Still, a Canton *Ledger* would know few stings more painful than if a neighboring, bigger competitor—in Canton, the metropolitan Peoria *Journal Star* would qualify—beat it with local news, especially something gigantic. "I never fear that," Woods said. "We do what *we* do. We're local. We live here. We care about this community and the surrounding communities. I never fear what they [outside competitors, not specifically the *Journal Star*] are going to do."

"Rumors were starting to get out, what might happen," Meade said. He and the few others in the know did everything they could to keep the secrecy, but mysterious things were passing through City Council votes, and newspapers cover those things. *Journal Star* reporter Matt Buedel had come the closest to public revelation. Four days ahead of the church ceremony, he wrote in his newspaper: "Officials in Fulton County's largest city are on the verge of announcing what they deem a major economic development project that will be located on the former International Harvester site."

December 11, 2008, was a day that Canton will never forget.

Just ahead of that, Meade had wanted to start a buzz. He let the word spread in Canton about a big announcement coming at an event to be held on the upcoming Thursday afternoon. At First Baptist Church. Across from the IH site. And still two and two weren't adding up to four for most of hope-dimmed Canton.

That morning, another Matt Buedel Peoria *Journal-Star* story tipped the hand, under the headline: "Manufacturing business coming to Canton." A press invitation to the ceremony was Buedel's source. Still, Meade, Rothert, and others involved feel strongly to this day that most of the audience in the church came in unsure of what they were about to hear. "The whispers had gone all around town," Linda Woods said. "Word had gotten around a little bit," Mike Walters says. "I didn't see a factory coming at all. I thought maybe Mr. Cook had bought another building downtown, there was going to be something renovated, and that would be it."

It was the once-burned, twice-shy adage multiplied. By then, Canton had felt too many burns to jump to even the palest of rosy conclusions about that site and its future. "We were devastated," Walters said. "Our community knew we were at a junction that wasn't going to be good. Just about everybody thought: What is going to come in *here*? We've got an eyesore right downtown—not only an eyesore, a place you can't even build on. Right downtown! It's always going to be empty. We're always going to have that eyesore there. And we have eyesores on the square around it."

Meade and his "brain trust" had spread some word about a big announcement and hoped that would be enough to get an audience, because they knew—and only they—that Bill Cook was coming himself to make the commitment. Carol Davis was in that inner core as head of the Spoon River College Foundation, and she urged everyone she saw at the school to get there. "Her fear [they learned later] was that Mr. Cook would be coming in and there would be only a few people at the church," said Tracy Snowman, a faculty member who went.

Oh, Canton came that day. And came, and came, and came. The sanctuary filled quickly, then the balcony. "It got so crowded we started worrying about that balcony," Snowman said. So did Meade, and church officials. But, it held.

Estimates on the total turnout, counting people standing outside and across the street, run above 1,000. Chrissie Peterson says 2,000. How does that happen in a small town on a December Thursday afternoon? "You know, I don't know," Peterson said. "People left work. People left school. I think everyone just knew it was going to be a pretty substantial Cook project."

"That was the magical day," Tony Rolando says, "that day at the Baptist Church."

As the place was filling, Bill and Carl Cook, with Jim Murphy and Scott Eells, entered down the center aisle and took reserved front-row seats, arriving without fanfare, without applause. "I didn't know him by sight," Tracy Snowman said. "I was trying to figure out which one he was. As usual—incognito, sweater, no suit, no tie, just a very ordinary person in Canton."

Before there was an announcement, there was a point in the program when Bill Cook was introduced. He stood, turned toward the crowd behind him, and gave a wave. "That turn-around wave—oh my gosh!" Linda Woods says. "That was the pinnacle." Without mention of a factory or anything else, Mark Rothert remembers, "They introduced Bill, and everyone just clapped, for a long time. Everyone in that room that day had to have had a family member who had worked at Harvester on that site, or had some emotional attachment to that site. That's what brought so many people there—that ground is somehow hallowed in the minds of people of this community. It runs all the way back to the beginning of this community, in the 1850s. They knew Mr. Cook was there for a reason. He stood up, and everyone just stood . . . and clapped—a standing ovation.

"Choke up? Oh, yeah, I did. My dad and my grandpa worked at that site. It was very emotional for me, to be a part of all of that."

And then the program began.

Matt Buedel's Peoria *Journal-Star* story the next morning captured the day:

> CANTON—to understand the heartbreak wrought by the shuttering of International Harvester 20 years ago and hope ignited by the prospect of another manufacturing Center on that hallowed property, one had to look no farther than the First Baptist Church on Thursday.
>
> Nearly 1,000 people packed the sanctuary and an overflow space directly across Elm Street from the now-barren 38-acre tract that once represented the very pulse of Canton and Fulton County. Parking was scarce; inside seats were more rare.
>
> They came to confirm what many of them already knew: Bill Cook, a Canton native who had made a fortune crafting medical devices in Indiana, was unveiling his newest venture—a factory that would join his empire under the auspices of the Cook medical company.
>
> And amid all the superlatives state and city officials used to describe the project and the bureaucracy-busting efforts out of which it was born, those people proved the emotion a community has invested in land that seemingly touched every resident's life.
>
> After wide-screen televisions on either side of the pulpit flashed with 'Cook Canton,' the name of the new plant to be built on what is more informally known as the IH site, several people in the audience wiped back tears. The calm that followed a boisterous standing ovation was punctuated by a chorus of sniffles.
>
> "We can finally start the healing process on the IH closure and fire," declared Mark Rothert, executive director of the Spoon River Partnership for Economic Development.

A GATEHOUSE NEWSPAPER

Journal Star

FRIDAY
DECEMBER 12, 2008

$1.00

SERVING CENTRAL ILLINOIS SINCE 1855

www.pjstar.com

'PLANTING A SEED' IN CANTON

Plans announced for new plant on the former International Harvester site

DAVID ZALAZNIK/JOURNAL STAR

Bill Cook, left, joins applause during Thursday's news conference announcing plans for the Cook Canton medical equipment manufacturing plant. Cook, a former Canton resident, is founder and chairman of Cook Group Inc. At right is his son and company vice president, Carl Cook. Between them is Jim Murphy, president of Cook Financial.

BY MATT BUEDEL
OF THE JOURNAL STAR

CANTON — To understand the heartbreak wrought by the shuttering of International Harvester 25 years ago and hope ignited by the prospect of another manufacturing center on that hallowed property, one had to look no farther than the First Baptist Church on Thursday.

Nearly 1,000 people packed the sanctuary and an overflow space directly across Elm Street from the now-barren 33-acre tract that once represented the very pulse of Canton and Fulton County. Parking was scarce; inside seats were more rare.

They came to confirm what many of them already knew: Bill Cook, a Canton native who had made a fortune crafting medical devices in Indiana, was unveiling his latest venture — a factory that would join his empire under the auspices of the

Please see **CANTON**, Page A7

Canton Mayor Kevin Meade addresses the overflowing crowd Thursday in First Baptist Church of Canton, where plans were announced for a new plant on the site of the former International Harvester in Canton.

DAVID ZALAZNIK
JOURNAL STAR

Front page Peoria *Journal Star* on announcement day.
Journal Star *photos by David Zalaznek.*

Meade's predecessor as mayor, Rod Heinze, said, "A dark cloud has been lifted off Canton and now there will be blue sky. We can look up and the sun is shining through. This is real. Thank you, Bill Cook."

Meade said, "For 25 years, the city of Canton has been bypassed by economic growth while the nation prospered. Now it is ironic that things are going the other way. We can now say to our children, 'You have an opportunity.'"

He called the 69 days since the Cook call "a whirlwind," during which all involved were "doing things we were told were impossible to do, unheard of in the state. We bent some rules, all legal of course . . . Cook likes to do business quickly. They are a leader in their industry, doing $1.5 billion in business. They employ thousands worldwide. Many second and third generations of families work for them because they take care of their employees.

"They decided to build in Canton because we represent Midwestern ethics and values. We will always remember and honor our past, but the time is now to move beyond International Harvester. To quote Churchill, 'This is not the end. This is not the beginning of the end. This is the end of the beginning.'"

Meade mentioned those hallowed names of Canton's past: Parlin, Orendorff, Ingersoll among them. "Today the Cook name joins them."

Except for the introduction, Bill Cook never left his seat. "I kept watching him through the whole thing," Tracy Snowman said. "I could see he was thrilled, but he never carried a self-importance. It was like, 'Wow! I'm glad they're liking this!'" Scott Eells, the Illinois-born 6-foot-9 former Indiana University basketball player who is the top man in manufacturing in the Cook organization, spoke for Bill and told the crowd the Cook company would be investing more than $5 million in the factory.

"We think it will fit very nicely into the neighborhood," Eells said. "We are very excited to be part of rebuilding Canton. The community has embraced us and has been very eager to be part of our development."

Then Eells put his finger on a piece of the entire Cook-to-Canton tale that truly was a miracle: "It has also been a pleasure to work with Mayor Meade and the state of Illinois."

"BRAIN TRUST" GOES TO WORK

Of all those hurdles that came up that day in Mayor Meade's office, the most imposing figured to be rushing anything through Illinois state government, renowned for its red tape.

It's all still a blur even in the mind of the woman who first brought the problem up, City Attorney Chrissie Peterson. Immediately after that nothing-but-yes Monday in Meade's office, she says, everybody went to work: "Mark Rothert on writing a grant for the Illinois Department of Transportation for the road we would need, and to the Federal Economic Development administration; the City Engineer, designing a road, water lines, sewer lines, storm sewer lines, figuring out how to get concrete crushed and removed; Tony Rolando, writing a CDAP [Illinois' Community Development Assessment Program] application for funds that we could use to offset some of the infrastructure costs; Carol Davis, on helping job applicants." An Illinois law required a testing step that would have cost each applicant almost $25. Davis lined up state aid that covered the cost for the first 600-plus applicants.

"And I went to work on all the other stuff," Peterson said, "subdividing plats, working with International Harvester, working with the insurance companies, working with EPA . . . When we wrote the CDAP grant application, we were told by the state that it could never be done in two months, that it took at least twelve months. The mayor said, 'Tell me who the best grant writer in the state is.' We found her and hired her.

"We had to get signoffs from all the various state agencies, EPA, Historic Preservation, Department of Natural Resources . . . We stalked those poor people on the phone, by e-mail; at one point the mayor was in Springfield standing outside people's offices to get signatures."

Tony Rolando says, "A lot of my job was to get funding for the city to build streets and infrastructure for the plant." Exhibit A that he succeeded is Third Avenue, Canton's newest street, a thoroughfare that passes by the Cook factory site. "I don't think it ever existed, because it's where the plow works was," Rolando said. "Now it's the best street in town."

The No. 2 man in the state agency that Rolando represents is Warren Ripley. "Wonderful guy," Rolando said. "I had told him about this. I said, 'Mr. Cook's company is private. He's not going to give us all the financial data you want.' He said, 'It's not us trying to be nosy. By law, we have to see it to get this tax credit. I'll make an exception. I've only done it one other time. We'll accept a redacted copy of it, for a file, as long as they will bring it to us if there's a problem.'" The Cook company set aside its own operational rules and obliged. "Somebody had to fly to Springfield with a briefcase full of documents from Cook," Peterson said. "They wanted to know where Cook's debt schedule was. They were told, 'There isn't any.' They all laughed and asked if they could apply for jobs."

And there was the mayor. Cook president Kem Hawkins watched the Canton doings from afar and said, "Things happen because of certain leaders. Kevin Meade is one such leader. If something needed to be done—zoning, or anything—he was on it, and it was done, and it was signed—and bam!"

Carl Cook still marvels at Meade's ability to deliver on his 69-day sprint. "Illinois is a state of road-blocks, and he just mowed those down," Cook said. Meade passes credit along to Tony Rolando: "He knew people at the state level and guided us to the right people." Mark Rothert tamps the miracle stuff down just a bit. "It was 2008—the whole national economy was in the tank, the bail-out of financial institutions was going on," he said. "Government agencies at the state and federal levels were looking for any really positive project. This absolutely represented that. They were easy to convince to get behind it with grant money they had available."

And still there was a last-minute only-in-Illinois problem.

"Before we formally announced the project, Governor Rod Blagojevich had to sign off on one last piece of paper," Peterson said. "He and his representative were supposed to be here." On December 9th, two days before the announcement, federal charges were filed against Democrat Blagojevich for allegedly putting up for bid—the Justice Department considered it soliciting a bribe—the U.S. Senate seat that Barack Obama left to become President.

"He got arrested December 10th—the day before our event," Peterson said. "It did send us into a bit of a tailspin. We said, 'Two thousand people are showing up tomorrow. What are we going to do if we don't have that piece of paper?'"

Just in time, that paper appeared, sent "from somebody in Springfield," Peterson said. "It has his name on it. I would assume somebody had a stamp."

At lunch on the day of the announcement, Carl Cook recalls, "I sat beside one of the state representatives. The topic of the governor and his issues came up, of course, and I said, 'I read in the paper this morning that the way the state constitution reads it will take them two or three months to impeach him, let alone try him.' And this guy—who was a Democrat—said, 'We'll have him out by Monday afternoon.' And that's exactly what happened."

"This guy" was Rep. Mike Smith, the Speaker of the House. Rolando translated, "the consummate Chicago politician—he gets things the way he wants them. They wanted Blagojevich out and they got him out."

Months later, Meade remembered what he saw from the First Baptist pulpit that day: "The people of Canton had turned out . . . the looks in their eyes and tears on their cheeks were pure joy. They knew that the spark this town needed had just arrived."

"People were actually crying," Mark Rothert said, "at the announcement and afterward."

"I did get the impression most of the citizens didn't know ahead," George Ridgway said. "That was an emotional meeting."

Mike Walters never will forget walking out of First Baptist Church into the sunlight of that day. "I thought, 'Man! This is great! Wow!' It seemed like the whole outside was different.

"If you would have asked me who Bill Cook was before 1995, I'd have said 'I don't know.' Ninety-nine percent of the people in Canton would have said, 'I don't know him.' The people who went to school with him knew him, yes, but not many else. And this man who 99 percent of the people didn't even know said, 'I still love Canton. The need is here.' And here comes Bill Cook, not with hundreds of dollars—millions! How many people from anywhere who leave and make it big ever even think of doing something like that?

"The man helped us tremendously. He gave us hope. He gave us life.

"It gives me a great outlook on where we're headed. Now, the community's getting help from everybody. There really is a Canton."

The teary-eyed and the smiling, the visiting politicians and the man who had caused it all, everyone moved outside from the church across the street for the formal ground-breaking. With gold shovels.

Right then, someone had the perfect thought. Canton suddenly heard a sound it hadn't heard since that dreadful Christmas Eve closing. The IH whistle blew.

There was a time, Meade said later, "when our lives were regulated by the IH whistle. It was our life." It wasn't a big whistle, but its noise was huge. Hence, its nickname: "Big Toot." Mike Walters described it in *Legacy:* "41 inches high . . . mounted atop a steel pipe 50 feet long. It took 9,000 pounds of steam per hour (300 horsepower) for a continuous blast. Legend said it was identical to one that sank with the U.S.S. *Lusitania* in 1911."

Every corner of Canton heard it when it blared. Every work day it sounded seven times:

6:00 AM as a wake-up call for employees
6:52 to signal eight minutes left to get to work
7:00 AM, starting the work day
12:00, high noon, starting the lunch hour
12:22, eight minutes left before work resumed
12:30, start of the afternoon shift, and
3:30, end of another day.

Two other times each year it sounded. The first was at 11 AM each November 11th, the 11th hour of the 11th day of the 11th month—the moment in 1918 when the armistice was said to have been signed, ending World War I and giving America Armistice Day and later, as wars continued and more valiant soldiers died, Veterans Day—that IH whistle blared for one stirring, memory-provoking minute. The second, at Midnight on New Year's Eve—Canton people could set their clock on it—for one full minute, that whistle shrieked a triumphal, year-welcoming blast.

"That whistle was life itself," Meade said.

When the burned and abandoned factory shop was razed, the whistle was saved. It resides atop the Canton City Building. And Canton learned that December day in 2008: "Big Toot" still works.

"THE STORY OF THE CENTURY"

Meanwhile, on the day of the big announcement, there was the saga at the Canton *Ledger.* That Thursday afternoon, when the story *was* a story, the *Ledger,* not its bigger-city rivals, had it first. And, in Nathan Bedford Forrest terms, "furstest with the mostest" wins.

Small papers give away lots of advantages but retain one edge. Flexibility. Their deadlines aren't essentially dead. Ordinarily, Linda Woods said, "We try to get the paper to the press around 10 o'clock in the morning. That day we just made it a point to go when we had the story. We told our publisher at the time [Scott Koon] what we wanted to do, and the motor-route drivers, of all people, were giving him fits, so he came in and tried to talk us out of waiting.

"I told him, 'You know, this is the story of the century around here. Just give us some time.'"

Facing. Front page Canton *Daily Ledger.* The Story of the Century.

Canton, Illinois

The Daily Ledger

97th Year – Vol. No. 61

Thursday, December 11, 2008

WEATHER -- Tonight: Mostly cloudy with a 40 percent chance of light snow. Lows around 20. Northwest winds 5 to 10 mph. Friday: Becoming partly sunny. Highs in the mid 30s. Northwest winds 10 to 15 mph. Friday night: Mostly cloudy. Near steady temperature in the lower 20s. South winds 10 to 15 mph.

It's about YOU

75¢ per copy   Look for our online edition: www.cantondailyledger.com   Fulton County's Home Newspaper

WELCOME HOME, BILL COOK

Cook offers Canton jobs, hope

CITY OFFICIALS, RESIDENTS, DIGNITARIES CELEBRATE DAWN OF NEW ERA WITH NEWS OF MEDICAL DEVICE FACTORY FOR FORMER IH SITE

By JOHN FROEHLING
of the Daily Ledger

Bill Cook, who grew up in Canton and went on to build the largest privately owned company in the world due to his success in the production and sale of medical devices, has offered to buy property on the northeast corner of the old International Harvester site. He plans to build a factory that makes medical devices there and eventually employ more than 300 people there.

Canton City Council, after reconvening a recessed meeting this morning at the Historic Depot, opened a lone sealed bid for the purchase price and use of 7.5 acres of property deemed "clean" at the IH site. The bid was from a company called Cook Company Inc. Bill Cook, founder of Cook Group Inc., which is based in Bloomington, Ind. where he

resides, was on hand for the bid opening. He was recognized by the officials.

City Clerk Nancy Whites opened the proposal and reported the bid price was $100 for the property -- which the state Environmental Protection Agency has designated as needing "no further remediation." She said the proposed use was a manufacturing facility that would produce medical devices.

The time frame bid for bringing the property into use was the fourth quarter of 2009 or first quarter of 2010. The bid also proposed investing $5 million within years of the date of acquisition of the property and employing 150 people within that period.

Council then adjourned and walked to the First Baptist Church, which is located across Elm Street from the IH site, for

a special celebration which included speeches by the mayor, other elected local and state officials, the chief operating officer of Cook Group and representatives of state agencies.

Then a groundbreaking ceremony was held in front of the IH site. The old IH whistle blew at length at the end of the ceremony. A reception next was planned with refreshments at the church. Church member John Wertman was on hand on a volunteer and said his wife had made 113 dozen cookies for the occasion.

Scott Ellis, chief operating officer for Cook Group, said during his remarks at the church that the factory will first employ 50 to 75 people and "build as quickly as we can" to have in excess of 300 employees. He held an artist's rendition of the Cook facility planned in Canton and said it will cover 45,000 square feet. It is hoped to be built by next fall.

He explained later the local facility will start out by making "vascular introducers," or tubes that go into blood vessels to allow medical devices such as stents to be inserted into those channels. "That is a good product to start training people in a highly regulated field," Ellis said. "The development pipeline is very full. We'll look at adding other things as we go along."

According to press releases, job applicants must apply through the Workforce Investment Board/Career Link and Spoon River College and complete a testing and screening process. Recruitment for positions will begin by June. Information will be forthcoming on applications and application screening through the college and CareerLink. Updates on the project's progress may be viewed online at www.cantonillinois.org.

Mayor Kevin Meade noted earlier in a private interview with the Daily Ledger that Mark Rothert, executive director of Spoon River Partnership for Economic Development, wrote a letter to Cook in July 2007. (Both that letter and Cook's reply letter appear in their entirety in today's edition of the Daily Ledger.) Cook responded, thanking Rothert and inviting him to visit Bloomington, discuss prob-

lems of Canton, and see what has happened in the last 25 years in Bloomington.

Meade and Rothert both went to visit Cook, and Meade continued to do many trips to Bloomington at any opportunity when he was traveling in Indiana. Meade often traveled in connection with his job.

Cook came to Canton last summer as the special guest at the Spoon River Partnership's first annual dinner event. Cook talked about his business and announced he planned to purchase and renovated the historic 1883 Randolph building and adjacent building to the north on the east side of the Canton square. More recently, Cook purchased properties damaged by fire two years ago at 138 through 148 N. Main St., located just south of a city-owned parking lot on the southwest corner of Main and Locust streets.)

Meade said he got a call from Cook in September. It was an eventful telephone conversation. Cook asked Meade to tell him about the IH site and send him a plat of the property.

Meade drove to Cook's office in Bloomington, Ind., the next day. Cook told him he was thinking of building a plant in Canton but was concerned about being able to staff it with at least 300 workers.

Continued on A-6

Cook is welcomed by dignitaries

By LARRY ESKRIDGE
of the Daily Ledger

Speakers at First Baptist Church regarding plans of Bill Cook to build a medical-device factory across the street at the old International Harvester site spoke to a packed house as they offered a vision of a positive future for Canton.

"What a fabulous crowd," said Carol Davis, a vice president at Spoon River College, as she welcomed the 450 people in the sanctuary and noted an overflow crowd in Fellowship Hall downstairs viewing a broadcast of the event on screen. Some estimated the crowd to be around 600 people.

"This is a monumental and emotional day," she continued, thanking the First Baptist Church for hosting the event in their church, which was built in 1853. She then introduced a video production detailing the history of the International Harvester site from its beginning as the site of a blacksmith shop in 1840 by William Parlin and partner R.C. Culton to the present.

Davis then introduced Mayor Kevin Meade, who noted that as mayor, "there are good days and there are bad days. This is a good day."

Meade reflected on Canton's past, when "our lives were regulated by the IH whistle. It was our life. Twenty-five years ago, our lives changed. It was more than a plant moving, it was life itself."

Meade then introduced former Mayor Don Edwards, who was in office at the time of the closing of IH in 1983, the fire there in 1997, and redevelopment efforts that started after that, saying he was proud to have him there. "Economic development has been the focus of the city since then.

"There were a few rays of hope, but the fire let us know we have to start over," Meade said.

Meade noted past development prospects for the site included a theater and a restaurant, but nothing materialized of those plans.

In April 2008, Meade was invited to join a group of local pastors, including First Baptist Church Pastor Keith Jones, who had been praying over the site, and Meade said he wondered what he could offer them.

Continued on A-6

Photos by Bill Burnham
News of jobs will usher in hopeful future
Above, entrepreneur Bill Cook acknowledges the crowd during the ceremony announcing the planned construction of the Cook® Canton plant on the old International Harvester site. At right, shovels stand ready for the groundbreaking ceremony with a sign designating the site as future home of Cook Medical.

FUTURE HOME OF COOK MEDICAL

Photo by Bill Burnham
Cook Canton is announced
Canton native Bill Cook enjoys an ovation from the packed Sanctuary of the First Baptist Church in Canton, where the announcement of a new medical devices plant to be erected on the site of the old International Harvester. Cook is also responsible for reconditioning the old Randolph Building in downtown Canton.

Churches play important role in the good news

By LINDA WOODS
Executive Editor

"We walked along Elm Street (at the former International Harvester site) and decided to do something to beautify the site in hopes of bringing jobs and lifting the spirits of Canton residents," says Rev. Keith Jones of First Baptist Church.

That was one year ago.

Today, the church hosted a celebration and the announcement that Canton native Bill Cook will construct a medical device factory at the northeast corner of the site - the first to break ground there. It is expected the plant will support about 300 jobs.

Jones explains that he and several other Canton ministers (and their congregations) offered prayer at many times for jobs and for that site.

Canton ministers Kenny Bloyd (United Church of Christ), Jim Book (1st Church of the Nazarene), Michael Brooks (St. Peter's Episcopal Church), Kevin Kessler (Church of the Brethren), Maureen Stein (Trinity Lutheran Church), and Kevin Van Tine (Covenant Community Fellowship), were all part of that group.

At that time, Jones says no one even knew of any discussions with Bill Cook and his companies.

"We did make it (bringing jobs) a matter of prayer," says Jones.

Jones says that Canton residents have been "in mourning" for the lost IH plant and the jobs it offered and the group of ministers wanted to lend encouragement and offer hope.

Continued on A-7

It's a great day in Canton

Kevin Meade

Canton Mayor Kevin Meade explains, "Since the closing of International Harvester in 1983 and the devastating fire in 1997, we have been dedicated to revitalizing this historical site. This is a great day for Canton and the surrounding communities. While so many are suffering from economic loss, our region is blessed to have former Canton resident and entrepreneur Bill Cook and family invest in Bill's hometown."

Meade emphasizes, "The Cook name will join the historic Canton names of Parlin, Orendorff, Ingersoll, Coleman and Graham as examples of those who invested in our community and have enriched the lives of generations to come."

Mark Rothert

Mark Rothert, executive director of the Spoon River Partnership for Economic Development, said the positive impacts of the project could not be overstated.

These include:

-Hundreds of new stable and good paying jobs with great benefits.

-Having a company in the community that does $1.5 billion in sales worldwide annually.

-Revitalizing of a brownfield site.

-Increased potential for spin-off growth and development.

-More philosophically, we get to start the healing process over the traumas of IH's closure and fire.

"It's also just as important for us to celebrate what these jobs will mean for the individuals who get them," Rothert said. "Canton is home to many proud people who want to make a better life for themselves and their families. Some are single parents, some work hard at more than one job and still can't make ends meet, some drive to another county every day, others are underemployed and not reaching their potential. For them, the security of a job at Cook Canton can end many of their worries. For them this is truly life changing.

Continued on A-7

The December 11th edition of the Ledger is a keeper for all time, the edition that will go alongside the landmark editions all newspapers keep: Pearl Harbor, the Kennedy assassination, the moon landing. Maybe ahead of them, because this story was Canton's.

When those presses finally rolled, when those motor-route carriers delivered their papers a little before dinner on Thursday night, not Friday morning when the *Journal Star* big-time coverage came out, all Canton had a *Ledger* with a page one that carried four headlined stories and three full-color pictures, the largest in the upper right corner showing Bill Cook, with a broad smile, acknowledging the applause from the crowd in the church. And inside was a page with 13 color photographs from the day, including an artist's sketch of what the factory would look like. All of it was led off by front-page headlines that screamed:

WELCOME HOME, BILL COOK

COOK OFFERS CANTON JOBS, HOPE

The story of the century.

CANTON TODAY

There's not just a new look in Canton these days, there's also pretty much a different cast—in City Hall and the old "Brain Trust," anyway.

Mayors go up for re-election every four years in Canton. For Kevin Meade, after a little more than a term in office, that day was April 9, 2013, and the next day's *Daily Ledger* headline read:

FRITZ NAMED NEXT CANTON MAYOR.

Jeff Fritz, who had come to Canton from suburban Chicago in 2006 to serve as police chief, polled 1,163 votes to 1,109 for Meade, with 376 to the other entry in the three-man field, Steve Cape. In Canton elections, there are no political parties, no primaries, no preliminaries. The vote came in, and the Meade team went out.

"Seven years ago I'd never have told you I'd be involved in politics," Fritz said, sitting in his City Hall office four months after moving in. He grew up in the Chicago area, in Skokie and Morton Grove, and entered police work in 1976, serving two years in Elk Grove and twenty-eight in Bloomingdale. In July of 2006, a radical lifestyle change came when he moved to Canton as police chief under Meade's predecessor, Rod Heinze. Fritz served two years. In 2011, after leaving the department, he was elected alderman in his first try at politics. Two years later, he filed for mayor and won. In his early weeks in office, he said his alderman years "did help some, but I still have a huge learning curve."

He says he saw the change coming. "I had a couple of issues—I thought the administration here was top-heavy, and the police and fire departments were top-heavy as well.

"Each day I went out doing more and more canvassing, and I felt a little bit better. Around the three-month mark, I really felt like I was settling in. I never told anybody I thought I was going to win. I just said every day, as each day got closer, I felt better, a little more confident. I was going door-to-door. I was getting a lot of positive response—I know it's hard to say no to somebody in person, but you can read it. There are going to be those, 'Sorry. I appreciate you stopping by, but you're not my candidate.' But people were saying, 'We need a change.' It was 90 to 10.

"The reason I wasn't overly confident was I was going against an incumbent, who was a local resident. And then there was a three-way race. I was really concerned about splitting the vote, against the incumbent."

He was in Canton to see the whole Bill Cook effect on downtown. "Cook has been a great catalyst," he said. "It feels good to be part of this, going forward. What Cook has done helps out tremendously. I wasn't involved in it, but I got to see the first building built, then the second building. . . .

"I think the next major thing we need is to bring a four-lane road in. If we get a four-lane road here . . ."

"OH, WHAT A RUN"

The outcome was a stunner to Kevin Meade. All he kept hearing in his own campaigning, he said, "was, 'you've got nothing to worry about.' We had our poll numbers—they looked great, 92 percent approval rating. We said, 'OK, it shouldn't be a problem.' But we went out and worked—we didn't take it for granted. We had a thousand less votes than we had last time. In a town like this a thousand is a lot of votes." His conclusion: "It was just apathy—people were happy and didn't think they needed to go out and vote. You always have that percentage that isn't happy no matter what you do. We knew that would be 25 to 30 percent of the vote. Everybody who was happy stayed home. I *was* shocked.

"So how it's affecting me? My golf game's getting better, I'm spending more time riding my bicycle . . .

The new and the old. In front of the new Cook factory, a plow from the old days.

"I loved being mayor—one of the greatest experiences of my life—enjoyed it every day. I miss it, but . . . I didn't complain when I got elected and I'm not going to complain when I didn't.

"I think history will treat us very kindly and we'll look back and think, 'Oh, what a run we had.' We had about $150 million of new investment come into Canton in the last five years—that's over half a million dollars every week. Now, of course $50 million of it was Cook, but the other $100 million . . . I don't know what happened around the state, but I'll guarantee you per capita that's in the top five."

Meade's team is gone, too. Chrissie Peterson, though still a Canton resident, has joined a Peoria law firm. Another Cantonite, Nancy Rable is Canton's city attorney. Mark Rothert was gone before the election. He left shortly after the new Cook factory was open and into production, to become assistant county administrator for economic development for Peoria County. As he left, of course he looked back, of course he reflected.

"I'll always remember the downtown—what it was, and how it looks now. There's still more work that's going to happen, more streetscaping, trees and plantings and shrubberies—it's going to look even more esthetically beautiful.

"But right now it's greater than I've ever seen it.

"That's something I'll cherish about my time here, working with the Cooks on redeveloping downtown—the IH site, with the Cook factory there."

The Cook "factory" is now two new structures on beautifully landscaped land that so recently was so ugly.

And on the lawn of that lot, out front of the brand new, is something old, something time-honored, something classically Canton. It's not a statue, not a replica. "It's a horse-drawn plow," Jim Murphy says, "made by the original Parlen & Orendorff Plow Works."

THE PERFECT NAME

Mark Rothert doesn't underestimate the value to Canton of those eventful days that he and Kevin Meade's "brain trust" went through. "I really think the work the Cooks have done in the community, what the city has done, what we have done as community organizations—all of that has really changed the trajectory of where Canton was going to where it's going now. It took a lot of players to do that, all working together. Obviously, Mr. Cook was the major driver of all that.

"I hope this community never forgets that. We're way better off than we were just a few years ago."

Of all the changes in the beautified downtown, the hotel symbolizes things best for Rothert. "You have those main entrances into downtown—two directions, primarily, North Main Street coming from Farmington, and Route 9 on the southeast side, heading east toward Peoria. The hotel is right in the middle of downtown, so if you stay on either road you run into the hotel. And it's beautiful."

For many years on that site was a mural, essentially a portrait, of Col. Steve Nagel, a proud city's son, a highly decorated retired Air Force colonel and an astronaut who made four ventures into space and was commander of two of them, a genuine and legitimate town hero. But, Rothert says, "The building it was on burned down. So that building was demolished, and there was just a vacant lot there, and it was ugly."

At that point, and for a few years, "It was a terrible welcome into Canton," Linda Woods said. In its place is a handsome, inviting hotel called "The Harvester."

Now retired, Woods says "When I came to work, I came from North Main Street," Woods says. "Every day, I saw this hotel go up, and there was never a day it didn't make me smile. It's a thrill all over again, every day, just to look at the hotel—and to know what came before, and what after.

"Small-business people from this community now feel confident to open a business, join a group, and help make things happen. And now there are shoppers! People! People still go to Peoria, but the things that our little shops offer can't be found in Peoria, they're in Canton."

Amanda Holland, one of those "little shop" owners with her One East Boutique, joins Linda Woods' on her favorite route-to-work welcoming sight: "The hotel, always. It's a beautiful landmark. And I love the Snowmans' paintings."

Woods smiles. "That was Mr. Cook's aim: to get things started and have the people pick up. And they did."

Cook Medical president Pete Yonkman, who joined the Cook company as a young lawyer but stayed on in management, was executive vice president in charge of global sales and marketing in Bill's later years. Yonkman and Bill talked a lot, and Canton was a topic frequently enough to tell Yonkman what Bill Cook's hometown and its revival meant to him. "Bill put everything that he knew into Canton—in terms of business and community and philanthropy . . . the importance of business in a community and jobs in a community . . . how to renovate a downtown—not just put a bunch of money in it but how to get people involved, politicians involved.

"You think of how many small-town downtowns are dying. Bill was one of the few people who understood how to solve that problem."

"Bill just cared so much," Jim Murphy said. "He'd say, 'Murph, I want you to do this and this and this.' But he wanted people over there to be involved, not just us do it. So I was real careful to get other people into the fold and have them buy into this as well. And they did.

"The day we dedicated the murals, Tracy Snowman was speaking and got emotional, came to tears, because she talked about the renaissance of Canton. The beauty of that was that this was a citizen of Canton talking about the downtown coming back, with the influence of the Cooks."

That City of Canton website history talks of "the city's center square once again surrounded by historic buildings beautifully restored, lending a Norman Rockwell feel to Canton's primary business district." Canton is now "growing, and once again beginning to thrive—due to the generosity of a benefactor who chose to offer a hand up to his old hometown."

Old Canton and young Bill Cook. Old Bill Cook and new Canton.

"It *is* a love story," Tony Rolando said. "It really is."

And it continues, in new Cook hands.

In 2014, "Big Toot" came home. The classic whistle that had been a Canton symbol and staple so very many years returned to duty. Carl Cook made the

A new "Welcome to Canton."

decision, George Ridgway worked out the details, and in late-summer 2014 "Big Toot" was back in place atop a new factory on the old site, its work day trimmed down just a bit. Now it toots to open the day, signal the noon break, and mark the end of another work day.

Then there was Bill Cook's other aim: to bring cruisin' back to downtown.

"When they opened the Canton Square," Gayle Cook says, "Carl rode in a 1950s car with the mayor, to make the first loop around the square. It would have been Bill . . . but that was just great."

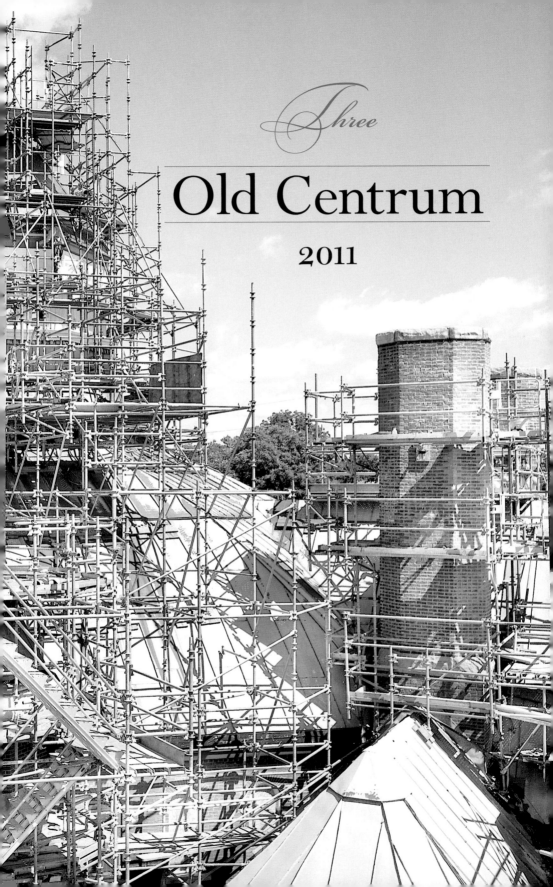

Three

Old Centrum

2011

"Bill got to see the stained glass, the sun was bright,
the organ played—everything was just gorgeous.
I remember Bill turned to Gayle and said,
'This was *worth* it!'"

—*Marsh Davis*

Previous page. A downtown Indianapolis landmark.
"Old Centrum" church in transition to new.

*M*aybe none of Bill Cook's restoration projects brought more of his particular interests into play than the route to recovery for the beautiful Old Centrum Church on Indianapolis's historic near north side.

Here was a place of architectural distinction with a history that warranted preservation, a sort of after-life of its own. It even has a dome. The building aged, yes, but kept its grandeur. To test its continued acoustical excellence, brass instruments blared. And, once its elegance was restored, it was ready to serve a valuable function.

Of course Bill and Gayle Cook jumped at the chance to rejuvenate the place and send it off into a new century with nobility of look and purpose.

It's at 12th and College, just northeast of downtown Indianapolis's heart. It is a heart itself, the hub of the city's historic Old Northside district.

The twenty-first is Old Centrum's third century. It was built in 1892, just in time to play a leadership role in the Social Gospel movement that had as its mission statement the portion of the Lord's Prayer: "Thy will be done, on earth as it is in heaven." Central Avenue United Methodist Church abbreviated neatly into Centrum, and when its spires were prominent in the city's landscape, its congregation's leadership was just as noticeable in pressuring that produced child labor laws and health care programs for the poor. The city's renowned Methodist Hospital has its roots there, as does Wheeler Rescue Mission. One of Indiana and America's most noted twentieth-century statesmen, former mayor and six-term U.S. senator Richard Lugar, grew up in the church, and as a child was baptized there.

"This was probably the pre-eminent Methodist church in its time, a very vibrant congregation," Marsh Davis, president of Indiana Landmarks, said. "Its heyday was a period of great social outreach in the church, not just for religious purposes. That's why the gymnasium was built. It was also an era of big Sunday Schools. It was a thriving, large congregation, until the post-war years, when a lot of the congregants moved north. St. Luke's [currently Indianapolis's biggest Methodist church], I understand, was largely an outgrowth of this church. But in its day, this was a happening place. Over time, it dwindled. Sometime along the way the Methodists officially pulled out."

When that happened, Davis said, "A non-profit organization formed called the Old Centrum Foundation—people who were concerned about this neighborhood and this building, with a purpose of sustaining the life of this building. They raised about a million dollars to repair it."

But that was nowhere near enough to save it. So, it entered the 2000s haggard, a "crumbling old building," in Davis's words.

His organization, Indiana Landmarks, describes itself as "the largest private statewide preservation group in the United States," its mission "to help Hoosiers save and restore old buildings." Indiana Landmarks is also the chief tenant in the new Old Centrum. There's a story there that runs—as do so many of these stories, be they in French Lick–West Baden, Canton, or Washington County—through Bloomington.

"A LITTLE DIM BULB WENT OFF"

Davis says the trail linking Old Centrum and Indiana Landmarks started in 2006 at "a dinner I went to at the Indiana Historical Society, at the grand palace they have, the Marilyn and Eugene Glick Center, right on the canal [in downtown Indianapolis]. I looked around the room and not all but many of the great philanthropists and civic leaders of Indianapolis were there. I began to feel a little blue: Why can't we get people to come to *our* place? And I realized, we don't *have* a place. We had a nice office, but small—we could barely get our board of directors into our board room.

"At the time, the church building was operated by the Old Centrum Foundation, and I got a call from them: 'We're out of money. We're going to have to shut this place down.'"

Two disconnected items, then: the dying church building and Indiana Landmarks' need for a home. Davis went into rescue mode for Old Centrum, but the people he tried to interest in saving the place weren't buying. "Somewhere in this process we [he and Landmarks executive vice president Tina Connor] started thinking: 'What if *we* took that on? Could we save that building and make it our state headquarters, and have a really great thing?'

"We knew it would take some very special philanthropy. Someone joked, 'Wouldn't it be great if the Cooks would be interested?'

"Right about then, Gayle Cook was giving a lecture at the first gala for the Monroe County History Center in Bloomington. Her topic was 'The

Mystique of Domes.'" It was a lecture augmented by slides of domes from throughout the world, including of course the Cooks' dramatic restoration at West Baden, Indiana.

For Marsh Davis, thinking of the upcoming lecture, "A little dim bulb went off: 'The Cooks have never done anything this far north, but Centrum does have a little dome. Maybe we ought to go to that event.' We bought a table. Judy O'Bannon [a Landmarks officer and widow of former Indiana Governor Frank O'Bannon] came with us. The goal was to get Bill and Gayle to come back and look at our little dome and see if they'd have any interest.

"And they did—about two weeks later they came up here. It was very cold. There's a lot of space between the ceiling and the roof. To get there we had to crawl up a really narrow, skinny ladder to a hatch. Bill and Gayle crawled up there and had to crawl on their hands and knees to get under the beams. They were really intrigued by it."

But not sold, in Davis's reading. "So now it was a question of how do we take it to the next level of interest? There wasn't a Plan B for this. We didn't have another plan outside Bill and Gayle."

There also wasn't the usual threat of imminent demise. The building's best years were behind it, certainly, and its salvation untold dollars away, but it was never on any endangered list, because up to then, as Davis said, "the Old Central Foundation had operated it." That support had ended. "We had a very touching hand-over of the property. They were glad to deed the property to us. Thrilled. They felt that they had accomplished their mission. They kept the building alive."

Marsh Davis's answer to the question of raising the Cooks' level of interest in Old Centrum was something he called a "cultivation event," to show off the building's exceptional acoustics.

Gayle recalls, "Tina and Marsh asked us to come up because they were having the acoustics tested in both the sanctuary and the theater." As "tests" go, this was a big-time event. Davis was ready: "Geoff Lapin, a friend of mine, cellist with the Indianapolis Symphony Orchestra, Mary Ann Tobias, a classical pianist and music scholar, and Zack DePew, our concert master here, formed 'The Landmark Trio' and we had a musical soiree. In addition to the Cooks we had Senator Lugar, Judy O'Bannon, Mario Gonzago, conductor of the Indianapolis Symphony, Jane Blaffer Owen from New Harmony, David Willkie from Dick Lugar's staff [and relative of 1940 Republican presidential candidate Wendell Willkie], and David's mother, Virginia Willkie."

Central Avenue United Methodist Church.
Always a treasure, but showing its age.

And the Centrum? "The building was really crummy at the time," Davis says, "smelled of dead mice, the ceiling had collapsed. We dragged in chairs and extension cords—we did it in what we now call the theater to check the acoustics" because, Gayle says, "It wasn't worth turning it into a performance center unless the acoustics were good."

The musicians' performance proved the acoustics' worth, which didn't surprise Davis. "When they built this, they didn't have acousticians, but they did have builders and architects who knew how to build things like Carnegie Hall."

There was more to the evening's sales effort than just that test. "Lugar talked at length about how this was his church," Davis said. "Then we went next door to the Morris-Butler House [the preserved Old Northside mansion of Noah Butler, the benefactor for whom Butler University was named] for a cocktail reception, and Bill talked with Lugar even further about it.

"I knew Bill was interested. He said something like 'If you can pull this off, I'll help you with some of the decorative painting—we'll bring in Conrad Schmitt and do what they call "The Mary Kay," to make it look good. You talk to Senator Lugar and have him get you some of that stimulus money.' I did call his office, but nothing happened.

"A few months went by. On November 9, 2009, we had what I called 'The Hail Mary' to try to get Bill really interested in this. We knew, of course, how much he [as the Tony- and Emmy-winning man behind the Broadway show *Blast!*] loved brass. We lined up ten brass players from the Indianapolis Symphony to play."

So the Cooks were invited and accepted. Then, Davis says, "At the very last minute . . . the traveling musical *Chicago* was playing in Indianapolis, and all of our brass players got gigs with it, so they were out for our date. But, my friend Geoff Lapin found four students from IU to come up and perform.

"This was scheduled for 2 o'clock on a Sunday afternoon. Bill was always early. We had Judy O'Bannon again, not quite as big a crowd as we had the first time, but the Cook people were there, Bill and Gayle, Carl, George Ridgway . . . 1:30 . . . quarter-till 2 . . . no musicians . . . 5-till 2 . . . I thought, 'This is it. We're screwed.'

"About 1 minute till 2 these four kids arrived, unpacked their horns, and it was spec-*tac*-ular! Just a *magical* event.

"Bill would say, 'I want to hear a trumpet fanfare,' and they would do it. Carl was upstairs, and Bill would say, 'Son, how're the acoustics up there?' 'Good, Dad.'

"After he'd had enough of that, he pulled me aside and said: 'Here's what I'll do: I'll do these two rooms [what is now called the Grand Ballroom and the Theater] and you do the rest.' I said, 'Bill, that's wonderful, but we can't do the rooms without the walls and the roof. It wouldn't make sense.' He said, 'No, I'll do all that—the roofs and walls. I'll take this part and you take the 1922 part [the last wing built onto the Rube Goldberg-ian structure, where Indiana Landmarks offices are now]. That'll be the deal.'

"We shook hands, there was never a contract or a budget, and away we went."

"CREEPING ELEGANCE"

Not long after that, Davis says, "George Ridgway was here and looked at the building, probably thinking, 'Oh, my God, what am I getting into now?' There were something like 24 different levels he had to rectify. There were three distinct sections: the original building in 1891, then in 1900 they built the Sunday school rooms with whole different levels. There were no federal regulations then: you just helped people up the stairs. A lot of stairs.

"Then in 1922 they added the last wing—probably for classrooms and offices. In the basement was a gymnasium that I was hoping to save, for neighborhood events and things," Davis said. "That didn't work out. We needed office space, a mezzanine, elevators, restrooms—the gymnasium got squeezed out."

Davis wasn't far off in guessing Ridgway's first-look reaction. It hadn't come at the acoustics test—earlier, in a private trip, Ridgway said. "Bill told me and [engineer] Greg Blum, 'I want to go look at a building in Indianapolis.' He pulled into the church parking lot and he said, 'This is it. This is the project.'

"It was pretty deplorable then."

It didn't take many looks, including an appreciation for the bizarre number of different levels that had to be dealt with in the construction, for Ridgway to know that "holding the cost line" would be difficult. After a thorough look:

"I told Bill I thought we could do it for $10 million. He said, 'What could make it go past that?'

"I said, 'Creeping elegance.'"

As in . . .

"If you hear the statement, 'wouldn't it be nice if. . . .' What comes after that is dollars. And Bill was the biggest offender."

As an example, the present building includes a first-class kitchen. "To give Bill credit, he never intended to build a commercial kitchen—at least, if it was going to happen, *he* wasn't going to build it," Ridgway says. "Well . . . Marsh Davis and Tina Connor took him out to lunch one day, and on the way back to Bloomington that afternoon, he told me we needed to put in this $400,000 kitchen.

So, Ridgway says, "$17 million later . . .

"We went over, just a bit.

"He did hold the line on some things. He told Landmarks, 'The site and the landscaping is your work.' It was a $3-million contract just to do the landscaping and paved parking."

No federal tax credits were sought for the project, so there was nobody peeking over shoulders on every decision made . . . right? "*Oh, yes, there was!*" Ridgway semi-shouts. "The City of Indianapolis had more organizations . . . To build that building and comply with the local historical regulations—it was stifling!

"We could comply with the Department of Interior standards in a heartbeat. But here they had the Old Northwest Association—had to get their approval for almost everything. And the Indianapolis Historic District—the building was 'designated,' so we had to have a 'Certificate of Appropriateness'—that's what they called it—on anything that could be seen from the street.

"I had to get a 'Certificate of Appropriateness' on a cylinder lock the size of a silver dollar. And—I'll be damned—I got it *turned down* because I didn't tell them what *color* the cylinder lock was going to be. 'Is it going to be bronze? Silver? Aluminum?' 'I don't *care.* I'll paint the damned thing *red*—whatever you want!'

"I think we had 80-plus 'Certificates of Appropriateness' we had to get. We put a metal cap on the top of the chimney, so water wouldn't run down through. 'What's it going to look like? What's it going to be made of? What shape's it going to be? What color is it going to be?'

"I said, 'Can't we do anything on a temporary basis and not have to get a Certificate of Appropriateness?' A woman on the board said, 'Well, yes, if it's going to be temporary.'

"I said, 'This is going to be temporary.'

"She said, 'For how long?'

"'For 60, 70 years—then you can have it back.'

"I got so frustrated that we hired an architect from a company up there who was an intern to do all *that* work, because I just couldn't put up with it. You have to replace windows, they need to look like what was there before—I understand that. You have to put new openings in the building—that needs to be approved. You have to close up openings—same thing.

"But, come on! The color of a cylinder lock? That you can't see from the street anyway, unless you have eagle eyes?"

The project fully met every Bill Cook precept about restoration leading to function, though where hotels returned as hotels in West Baden and French Lick and a mill as a mill at Beck's Mill, Old Centrum never was intended to return primarily as a functioning church.

"Bill's vision," Ridgway says, "was to move the home office of Indiana Landmarks into the building, restore the sanctuary and the small auditorium, and Indiana Landmarks could be financially stable because they would have a source of steady income: they could charge for meeting space, weddings, mass meetings, and events like that. They would still need donations, but everything they brought in as donation money could all go to restoring Indiana."

"Bill's vision" was a frequent topic of wonderment among his closest people. "Bill had that eye," Kem Hawkins once said. "Steve Ferguson put it beautifully: Bill always saw what it could be when he walked in. I would always see what it is. I could get there, but someone had to trigger me to get there. Bill had a knack of just seeing the world so differently, and reacting to the world so differently."

Once the work on the church had started, every Tuesday for weeks Bill made a personal inspection tour to keep up on progress at the site. "We both made 80 to 90 percent of those regularly scheduled weekly meetings," Carl Cook said. "I don't think there was ever one when we both missed."

"There was a huge rush to get everything done, fire inspection and everything, because we knew the day the doors opened [for the dedication program], it was going to be total capacity."

Tina Connor went through the transformative weeks with genuine *déjà vu*. She had seen this kind of miracle before. She represented Indiana Landmarks as project manager in overseeing the rescue of the West Baden and French Lick hotels. Part of her duty there was sticky: making sure "that nothing we were doing was going to be against preservation regulation. Bill didn't like regulation of any kind too much so that was a job."

But it did give her a close-up, week-to-week appreciation for both the man and the achievement. "I found him fascinating to observe. He was positive, a problem-solver, he liked fixing things, to make them work in the twenty-first century. It was a contradiction: he loved these old things but he also dearly loved figuring out where to put the elevator and how to make it work right—things it didn't originally have but needed today.

"So in some ways it seems a little odd that he was so interested in historic things. But he and Gayle—they were a team, and that was clear. She came here infrequently, when there was an artistic decision to make, about carpeting or wall colors. And you knew that she had done research behind the scenes. He really valued her contribution in that way.

"He wasn't about saving everything. Some of the things we wanted to save he called junk. He was very blunt. When people disagreed with him, he listened—he might not like it, but he had a respect for people who had an expertise, the craftsmen who do this work. He was always very complimentary when a journeyman carpenter or someone came up with a solution to a problem, in restoration."

At West Baden in particular, the rescue had been so dramatic. "It was just in dreadful shape," Connor said. "We had an expert that we rely on still, a real estate economist and developer from the East Coast, who told us in '95, 'We should call it a ruin and let people crawl on it.'" Indiana Landmarks never felt that hopeless, she says. "No, we never were. It's just such a fabulous place. But, golly, in retrospect if the Cooks *hadn't* agreed to help . . . it's such a big place and it was *so* dilapidated.

"At West Baden, in the beginning the Cooks said they thought it would take 12 to 14 million dollars. Then 20, then 25. They *must* have had conversations about the money they were spending. But the entrepreneur in Bill just wouldn't let him see a thing half-done, and not functioning. As it went along and you could see more and more progress, then I think he started being rewarded personally by witnessing it but also more and more people were telling him how wonderful a place it was and how great it was that he had stepped up. There *had* to be some personal gratification."

And all she can do is smile at the way Bill Cook himself had kept things going with the hotels, and kept raising his own personal bar of expectations, George Ridgway's "creeping elegance" factor at work. "Almost every week," Connor says, "I would come back to Indianapolis from West Baden and say, 'Guess what he's doing *now!*'"

West Baden: Indianapolis. With one difference: she sensed more of a push from Bill for a faster pace. "For everybody the timetable was very aggressive—it always was, but even more so there, I think. And they were working in an environment where, unlike Orange County, there was a lot of regulation. He didn't like that, and he didn't like that it was slowing things up. Because he wanted to see it done."

George Ridgway felt that unusual hurry-up push, too. "He had this drive all the way through, to get it done. I personally couldn't get things done fast enough for him."

Dedication Day, April 16, was coming.

"THIS WAS *WORTH* IT"

The dedication truly wasn't the new Old Centrum's first event. A request came in a few months in advance to use the beautiful sanctuary for a wedding a week before the opening. First instincts were to say sorry, it won't be ready, but Carl recalls "Someone said, 'It might not be bad to have a somewhat smaller event, and find out where the bugs are,' and I was thinking, '. . . provided we've got a bride who can understand you're going to be our test event—our guinea pig.'" There was an appropriateness to the test event. "The last event in Old Centrum before it really shut down was a wedding," Marsh Davis said. "The Old Centrum Foundation had basically decided they would do no more events. Then they said, 'All right, we'll open it up for one more.' The night of that wedding, a big chunk of the ceiling fell down—within hours of people having been there. It would have been deadly."

He didn't spread word about that near-miss widely, so the wedding of Matt Kirby and Julie Aud was approved for scheduling. Carl said, "I remember sitting in Dad's office one morning, he and Mom had been invited, and he said, 'Usually I don't go to somebody's wedding that I don't really know, but I think

Indianapolis's famed and historic "Old Centrum" today—a classic Bill Cook restoration: old glory retained for a new and living purpose.

I will go to this one just for fun.'" The Cooks knew they wouldn't be alone among strangers. Julie had worked in the office of Governor Mitch Daniels, and the Governor and First Lady were going. "They put Mom and Dad with the governor and his wife," Carl said. "They had a great time."

And the building passed every test—the solemnity of the occasion, the splendor, even the sound. Both Cooks went a-way struck by one part of the wedding in particular—soloist Lindsay Medina's singing of "The Lord's Prayer."

Dedication day.

Davis said he "crashed the wedding" in last-minute curiosity about how the building would look, and noted, "Bill got to see the stained glass, the sun was bright, the organ played—everything was just gorgeous. I remember Bill turned to Gayle and said, 'This was *worth* it!'"

Gayle Cook remembers, "We were just astounded at how beautiful it was, how well it worked. We went from the wedding across the hall to the reception. They had that decorated beautifully."

The Cooks drove back to Bloomington that Saturday night elated. Back Bill and his crew came on Tuesday for one more check-out, one more close-up look complete with Bill's sticky-notes on places that needed a last touch. Everything was on target as the grand dedication date countdown reached four days . . . three days . . .

Bill Cook was maintaining an altogether different, coinciding schedule. Dealing with his gradually worsening congestive heart condition was a constant part of his schedule. This was Bill Cook, intelligent and learned, one-time Northwestern pre-med student. Gayle Cook had always felt what he knew and understood about the human anatomy was a major reason why he had outlasted severe health problems. She had once said: "He knows when he needs something done, and he's aware of all the procedures that can be done. He has just done everything at every step. Someone else would have been gone long ago. Bill has always stayed just one step ahead. He knows when to have a check-up, and see if anything can be done—opening a vessel, whatever."

Elegance, from inside out.

Below. Inner Dome, Old Centrum.

That unusual insight and a few other things make it seem likely, in retro-spect, that by April 2011, Bill Cook knew his gallant 42-year fight against heart damage was about over.

"Fight" understates it. There were times his sheer will astonished the woman who knew him best.

OPENING DAY AT COOK HALL

Almost a full year before, April 25, 2010, was a highlight day in even as eventful a life as he enjoyed. That was dedication day for the athletic building he endowed for Indiana University—Cook Hall, a basketball practice and training facility that is best known for its handsome face: a two-floor museum memorializing the people, the events, and the history of IU basketball.

"One of the best speeches he gave was at the dedication of Cook Hall, and he could hardly walk that day," Gayle said. "Sometimes he was so weak, but you could just feel the adrenaline if he really wanted to do something."

Indiana University President Michael McRobbie was there, to acknowl-edge the $15-million Bill and Gayle Cook gift that had launched the project.

Below the honor gallery of photos of IU basketball greats,
early arrivals check out Cook Hall on its opening day.
Indiana University Athletics. Photo by Mike Dickbernd.

IU president Michael McRobbie has a
Big Red welcome for Bill Cook.

Gayle and Bill Cook, the people behind the
name, on Dedication Day at IU's Cook Hall.

Cook Hall Dedication.

So were IU basketball coaches Tom Crean and Felisha Legette-Jack, athletic director Fred Glass, varsity stars Jordan Hulls and Jori Davis, stars of another Hoosier era Quinn Buckner and Scott May. So was Steve Ferguson, ready to represent his long-time friend and associate at the podium during the program.

But Bill Cook did his own speaking. Without a note. Without a waver. Without a hint of what it took for a tired, drawn former athlete to meet that test. "I think he just felt, 'I can get myself pumped up,' and he did it over and over," Gayle said.

NO TIME FOR HINKLE

As Old Centrum's re-dedication day arrived, fifty weeks had passed since the one at Cook Hall. There was nothing else on the horizon, but there was a moment during that time when another restoration opportunity came Bill's way.

Barry Collier, athletic director at Butler University, was fresh off a Butler basketball season that had thrilled the nation—a totally unforeseen run by a representative of college basketball's "minor" leagues all the way to the 2010 national championship NCAA-tournament game. Collier's coach, young Brad Stevens, suddenly was a national darling. Collier hadn't announced it yet, but he felt the time was right to do something Bill Cook style: take Butler's 87-year-old basketball arena, historic Hinkle Fieldhouse, and spruce it up for a continuing lifetime of new service. The Fieldhouse had been built in 1927, so much ahead of its time in size (about 15,000 capacity) that it threatened to get the university in national hot water for overemphasis of athletics. Over the years, the place had taken on hallowed status in Indiana. It had been the site of more than 40 state high school championship games, including the one in the movie *Hoosiers* and in its real-world model: the 1954 state-championship game between little Milan and relative giant Muncie Central. Johnny Wooden played as a high schooler in that fieldhouse. And Oscar Robertson. All-time Hoosier high school heroes Larry Bird and Rick Mount never did get there in the state tournament but would have darn near died to.

Collier wanted to retain everything magical about the old place but to do it so it could stand and charm for another 80 years. Do what the Cooks did at West Baden and French Lick. He called a Bloomington friend and said, "Do you think Mr. Cook would be interested?"

"Do you have an architect?"

"No."

"Would it be open for George Ridgway to do it?"

"Oh, yes!"

After the conversation, the friend first ran into Ridgway, brought up the planned project, and asked, "Would you be interested?"

"That," Ridgway said, "would be like doing a cathedral."

The next stop was Bill Cook's office. The topic was outlined. The very quick answer:

"Nope. Somebody else will have to do that."

End of story. Firmly.

But why did the Bill Cook who had found such treasures in such less likely places, the Bill Cook who loved sport in general and the sport of basketball in particular, the Bill Cook who revered tradition and who had to know that in all of basketball-loving Indiana nowhere is more replete with it than Butler's 1920s field house, why had he said no?

Not that day but several months later, the question that ran through the questioner's mind was: Is it possible he already knew he wouldn't be around to see a project like that through? Had he measured his days and concluded Old Centrum was the last act?

If so, he measured very precisely, because in the terminology of another game, he carried that ball all the way down the field to the goal line, and let momentum carry it across.

At about 4:30 on the afternoon of Friday, April 15, 2011, less than 24 hours before the grandly preserved old Central Methodist Church was going to be officially opened and dedicated, Bill Cook died.

PART TWO

Measuring the Days

Death of a Giant

Bill Cook was alone at his home, on a couch in his upstairs bedroom, when he died at about 4:30 on the afternoon of Friday, April 15, 2011.

Gayle Cook thinks it's possible he had figured out in advance every element of that quiet passing, including its timing, and he wanted it just that way.

"He of course knew that it had been close for a long time," she said. "I think maybe that day he *did* know—maybe a week or so before."

Certainly, there were clues. His four-decade heart problem had reached the point where he had to go to Bloomington Hospital regularly to have fluid drained—a painful procedure called paracentesis (*pair*-uh-sin-TEECE-us). In Bill Cook's case, the process involved an anesthetic and an ultrasound machine. The man who never flaunted his wealth knew when to use it. After a procedure or two, he decided the hospital needed a whole lot better ultrasound machine, so he bought one as a donation. He supplied his own grit. "He was going once a week to the hospital, removing fluid that accumulates," Gayle said. "We did it in the morning, then he went to the office in the afternoon—every week, on a Friday. That had been going on for a year and a half."

That procedure had a uniqueness all its own. Bill Cook may have been its all-time record holder for times endured, and for days, months, and years kept alive.

His needs for it were exceptional. By high school everyone knows the human heart has two sides: the left ventricle and the right ventricle. Most heart attack victims "just have failure of the left side of the heart—that's where it happens," cardiologist Larry Rink says. "He clearly had that. But what was so unusual in his case—not rare by any means but people don't usually live long with it—is the right side also failed. Both sides, left and right, had failed. The significance of that is all the fluid from your body has to go to the right side of the heart. That pushes it to the lungs and then it gets to the left side. And usually you start getting what is called ascites fluid, and when you take that out, you lose some of the force that pushes it up into your heart, so your blood pressure tends to go down.

"With Bill, paracentesis meant we had to remove enough fluid to give him relief, but not enough to decrease his blood pressure too much. Then I would infuse protein back into his body [in the form of albumin], because protein tends to keep your pressure up. So I was literally measuring the amount of protein and sodium we took out, and then re-infusing the amount of protein we took out back in his body."

For years, he had been going to Cleveland Clinic periodically to have the procedure done. "At Cleveland Clinic when they did that," Rink said, "they put him in the intensive care unit and put catheters in his heart, measuring pressures, and taking this fluid out. Bill hated that. He did feel better after it, but he hated the procedure. The last time, he came back and said, 'I'm *never* going back up there again, and I'm not letting *anybody* put these catheters in.'"

With the Cleveland option shaky and Cook's need for the drainage steadily increasing, Rink investigated to see if he could do the procedure in Bloomington. There was an element of the pre-ordained: Rink had an unusual familiarity with the fluid/blood pressure problem that went way back—to his intern days at Parkland Hospital in Dallas. In 1966, after graduation from DePauw University and Indiana University Medical School, he was looking for a place to further him in his interests. He was steered not to Boston or Chicago or other metropolitan centers he had heard of but to Parkland, only a few years after the death of President John F. Kennedy was confirmed there November 22, 1963. "Parkland Hospital is part of Southwestern Medical School, which is very good," young student Rink learned. "When I was there, I was interested in this very area—hemodynamics, how this affects pressure—so the head of the department let me do a study to see how much fluid you could safely take out of somebody. There's not much in our literature about this but that's why I felt a little more comfortable about doing it with Bill."

The specialist who handled Cook's procedures at Cleveland Clinic told Rink it probably could be done in Bloomington, "Yeah, you could bring him in, put him in an intensive care unit, put all the catheters in, and do this, but you'll probably have to do it once every other week," Rink remembers. He also said, "We've never had anybody with this kind of procedure live more than three months."

Rink went to Cook with the Bloomington possibility and his first reaction was negative: "I'm not going to live that long. I'm *not* going to have that done."

"I convinced him to let us try a compromise procedure," Rink said, "do it more often, but do it without these central catheters. I told him it was going to take three hours, maybe once a week. That's basically what we did. We got him on a schedule. Sometimes we got off it because he wanted to go someplace, or he thought he felt good enough he could wait. But most weeks I would meet him at the hospital at 6:30 or 7:00 in the morning and get him all set. I wanted to just leave a catheter in and drain, but Bill knew that the risk of that is it can get infected, and he told me, 'I'm not going to survive if I get an infection in my abdomen.' He might have been right." So, another compromise: "We would put a needle in, then a catheter, but take it out each time.

"We started out draining about three liters—which is about three quarts—and then four. Pretty soon we had to do even more, because he would produce it so fast."

There was another complication. "His heart was expanded, too. All the medicines we use for that lower the blood pressure. It was an incredible balancing act, trying to get medicines to keep his heart from expanding more and yet keeping his blood pressure high enough that he could use his brain and his kidneys. Protein was a big deal for him—if the protein that floats around in your blood stream gets low, your osmotic pressure changes and fluid tends to leak out into your cells. Keeping the protein high tends to pull fluid back into his vessels . . . taking fluid out and infusing proteins back in—albumin, it comes in 12½-cc vials."

The week of the wedding at Old Centrum, the fluid withdrawal was exceptionally high: six liters, about a gallon and a half. "So," Rink said, "we removed six liters and infused 150 ccs [12 of the small vials]," with unsurprising ramifications. "That time his blood pressure went down and didn't come right back up." For the first time, he was held over an extra night at the hospital—released Saturday morning. And then he went right back to schedule, and made the wedding at Indianapolis that afternoon.

There was always one step between drainage and release. The procedure at Bloomington Hospital was exhausting for Cook, Rink said. "It all took several hours," Gayle said, "because he had to sleep before they would release him." Usually, post-procedure naps sufficed. That last time, Gayle recalls, "they did it on a Thursday [April 14], in anticipation of going to Indianapolis [for the Old Centrum dedication program] on Saturday. That was the second time that he didn't recover well—they couldn't get the blood pressure back up. They kept him overnight."

Friday morning, April 15, "his blood pressure still was not up," Gayle said. "He said, 'Well, I'm going home.' Larry Rink wasn't there; he was in China [associate Dr. John Strobel filling in for him]. Bill was determined to go, so he tracked Dr. Strobel down by phone, told him he was leaving, and got up and started walking down the hall. The nurses of course don't allow that—they're saying, '*Wait* a minute! *Wait* a minute! You can't *leave!*' [Daughter-in-law] Marcy's sister [Marta Young] was the nurse who usually took care of him. She went to the desk and said, 'No, no, no, you can't stop him. *I'll* go with him.' So she brought him to the car." The release records say that was 10:14 A M.

Gayle was waiting in the car. "I had no idea of this, that he was no better. [As they brought Bill to the car] I just thought he had recovered, as he had done for a year and a half.

"So he came home and he went to a chair."

A busy day had been planned, and once at home Bill Cook launched into it. His 11-days-younger cousin, Dr. Ivan "Van" Fucilla, Bill's close friend since childhood whose inside counsel as a Northwestern University medical school resident had steered Bill into the new medical thing called intervention, and his wife Judy were arriving from California that morning to attend the dedication on Saturday.

"Bill told me I would have to pick them up, that he didn't feel like going to the airport. Then he said, 'Take them to see Carl and Marcy and the baby.'

"And then bring them here?"

"No, take them to the Grant Street Inn and check them in."

"And then bring them here?"

"No, just let them stay there and we'll call them this evening."

Meanwhile, she says, "He had never gotten out of the chair, and I knew he was not feeling well. Normally, he would have been in the car and done all those things.

"So I did all these errands. Sometime, he went upstairs from the chair, lay down, and took a nap."

Thinking back, she reconstructed the morning.

"I'm sure he knew he was not recovering, and perhaps sent me away. He certainly knew what it means when you don't have blood pressure."

"I'm sure that he *did* know," Carl says, "just because something like that, he would sense. But I didn't sense that. He wasn't improving, but he wasn't necessarily getting worse.

"He hadn't felt good for a couple of days. And whenever he wasn't feeling good, he really just wanted to be left alone. Whether he had a sense of what was really going to happen, we'll never know. But I do know consistently throughout his life when he didn't feel good, he didn't want people around—'just go away and leave me alone.' Not in a rude way—just 'let me rest up.'

"Mom had told me that morning Dad was home from the hospital. I called him about 11:30. 'How's it going?' He said, 'I'm just going to rest up, then we'll do dinner tonight.'"

By then, Gayle was on her way to the Bloomington airport, where she picked up the Fucillas and got them to their hotel. She came home from there, in late afternoon, and discovered Bill, on the upstairs couch, lifeless. "And then I called 9-1-1."

In the Cook company headquarters on Bloomington's west side, officer Marty Deckard was ending his second week with Cook security, after a 22-year career with the Bloomington Police Department. Seconds after Gayle Cook's 9-1-1 call had been received at Police headquarters downtown, one of his former working partners, knowing Deckard's new job, called him to let him know a "man down, not breathing" call had just been received from the Cooks' house. Deckard called his superior, Dennis Troy, who had gone home to start the weekend at his Lake Monroe home.

"Within just a few minutes, there were 50 people here," Gayle said.

Vice-president Aimee Hawkins-Mungle, a close friend and confidant for both Bill and Gayle, also happened to be at home that afternoon, for an appointment "to meet the cable guy," she said. "Dennis Troy called my cell phone and said, 'I don't want you to panic, but it just came over the scanner that there's a possible heart attack at the Cooks' address. They're not saying his name, but that's the address.' I jumped in my car, and went straight to the house. When I got there, an ambulance was in front of the house and a cop car was in the driveway, two policemen sitting on the porch.

"I assumed Bill was having a heart attack. I went to a police officer and said, 'My name is Aimee. Just let Bill and Gayle know if they need anything, I'm right outside.' He said, 'Oh, wait a minute.' He walked inside, came back out and said, 'They're trying to find you.' I started up the stairs, and Gayle was at the top of the stairs."

One look told her the truth.

Gayle remembers clearly what she had found on her arrival home at about 4:30. "Bill was upstairs, lying on the couch. He had taken a shower, put a robe on, and lay down on the couch. He wasn't trying to call 9-1-1, he didn't fall over on the floor or anything, he just took a nap.

"I could tell he was not intending to go out to dinner that night. He had laid out pajamas. I'm satisfied that he was lying down, going to sleep."

Dr. Strobel was called to the scene in the role of coroner. He ruled that cause of death was "the heart muscle—that's heart failure, as opposed to heart attack," Gayle said. At last, after all those years, all those attacks, that muscle stopped responding. "You keep hoping each time that adrenaline gets you through," Gayle said. "And it did, for a long, long time."

Such a quiet ending to so momentous a life. And such a tumult it triggered in so many correlated lives.

One of those, right in the eye of the sudden storm, was Aimee Hawkins-Mungle. She personified the do-the-job, climb-the-ladder uniqueness of the company Bill Cook built. Like Tom Osborne, who arrived by motorcycle at the Cooks' apartment home as an eighteen-year-old and rose to the level of a Cook-labeled "genius" among the company hierarchy, and Phyllis Mc-Cullough, who answered a want ad and eventually became the company's first woman president, Aimee was a high corporate official without anything close to a college degree. One of Bill's last personnel acts was advancing her from his administrative assistant to vice president. Along the way she became tight-as-family friends of Bill and Gayle. It was a "close relationship," she says, "If they needed anything, anytime day or night, happy to do it. And Gayle still today."

All that factored into the multiplicity of roles Aimee found herself in as a quiet Friday afternoon turned into a chaotic evening. On those stair steps, she said, of course she and Gayle shared hugs and tears. "Once we got through the beginning of the emotional part, she looked at me and said, 'Now what do we do?'"

Aimee's shocked reaction was, "She wasn't kidding: he *hadn't* talked about his death. I thought he just didn't talk about it with us, at the office, but . . .'"

Gayle said, "What I was really saying was 'What do we do first?' Because Bill and I *had* talked about it. He had picked out the funeral music, he had picked the mausoleum . . ."

Aimee said, "Gayle and I gathered our thoughts, and started deciding what the plan was, moving forward."

Aimee, too, had "talked about it," and there was a plan, but it was a few miles away, in her office desk drawer, in Cook Inc.'s world headquarters. Much later, sitting in her office and thinking back, she said, "That's where I had thought it would happen, at the office—that was always in my vision: it would happen here, he wouldn't wake up from a nap . . ."

That quickly she was into the chaotic minutes that Bill Cook's closest associates in his business empire had feared were coming and sought to get ready for. She, Kem Hawkins, and Steve Ferguson had been talking and thinking in what-to-do-when terms "for about a year and a half, when Bill started getting really ill," Hawkins-Mungle put it. "When it happens, what is our plan of action as a company in notifying people?

"We knew it was going to be such a huge event, as far as trying to reach people. What do we want to say, especially to employees, who have been here for a long time and would be rattled, *very* rattled? We knew when it happened it would be very emotional. We devised a plan. We were trying to have something fairly ready to help us.

"I also started a personal file. So I had that plan in my mind: who I would call, being sure I didn't forget individuals who had meant a lot to Bill. I had all that—but unfortunately it was in my desk drawer, and I was at the house. We had to kind of reconfigure that.

"It worked out wonderfully, but it wasn't the way I had planned."

The first duty for Aimee Hawkins-Mungle was among the hardest: getting the word out within the company, to Bill Cook's closest of friends, a list made mentally, hastily, from personal knowledge and observation.

"When Carl and his family arrived, I took my phone outside to let them have their time. I called Dennis Troy and said, 'Yes, that's what's happened.' I called Kem Hawkins, and attempted several times to call Steve Ferguson. He was in French Lick, not answering his phone. So I finally got ahold of Connie [his wife] and didn't tell her what happened, just asked her to meet me at the house."

Bill Cook and Steve Ferguson: this was brother to brother, a friendship that started in the 1960s when they were introduced to each other at their wives' sorority party. Through the years, the bond grew stronger. Ferguson was a young attorney and exceptionally young state representative, Cook just beginning in his business. Ferguson did some legal advising and eventually joined the company. They began going together to sports events. Ferguson took Cook to the fabled Indiana state high school championships, Cook took Ferguson to Illinois's. "Then we started going to bowl games," Ferguson recalls. "And Super Bowls. We saw both of the Colts' Super Bowls. We went to Europe to see Scott May play.

"Drum Corps was always interesting. He wanted me to dress up in costume like him—the Roman toga, Uncle Sam. I never would. And when he shaved his head, he wanted me to, too. He'd say, 'Aw, come on . . .' and I'd say, "Bill, there's a *limit* to following you.'

"He just loved getting down to Cedar Farm—loved getting on a golf cart and taking people around. And traveling. In Europe, we walked and looked at downtowns—we walked every place we went in the world. In Germany, he liked the flowers downtown, and the window boxes. We came back and he said, 'What we want are window boxes downtown.' So we put window boxes on Fountain Square. Magnificent! Like downtown Europe.

"It's astounding the detail he could see. And the observations about people. You could be there with him in a room with 50 people, including family, and nobody would observe that something was bothering you. And Bill would say, 'What's wrong?' He used to tell me, 'When you get silent, I know you don't agree with me.' You might as well just say it, because he knew what you were thinking."

Steve Ferguson, the brother Bill Cook never had, was the main person Aimee set out to find, to make sure he knew before he heard it elsewhere.

When Ferguson finally got the message she had left on his cell phone, it was a simple directive that he clearly recalls: "Come quick." He didn't immediately think the worst. "I thought it was his heart again." The call sent him speeding toward Bloomington, about an hour trip. He was more than halfway there, "just north of Bedford," when by phone he got an e-mail message. From China. "Larry [Rink] had been keeping me informed," Ferguson said. "I got this e-mail from him that just said, 'Sorry, but there wasn't anything that could be done.'" That's how he learned.

At the Cooks' home, Aimee said, "While I was waiting for Steve, I started down my phone list [of other Cook officials]—George Ridgway, Pete Yonkman, Scott Eells, John Kamstra, Connie Jackson, some who were very close to Bill."

The message to each was as direct and as soft as she could make it. "I just told them, 'Bill is gone.' That's how I was phrasing it with his dearest friends.

"We were trying to get to as many as we could before they heard about it, but it wasn't just Dennis, everybody who had a police scanner was hearing it and telling their friends. After the first time, on the scanner they used Bill's name, and said he had passed.

"My cell phone—the text messages started going crazy. That's the other way I knew the word was out. By the time I got Jim Heckman [a vice president and long-time Bill Cook friend], he had already heard it. That was really upsetting for me. So I started asking people I called to call three or four people themselves.

"By then Steve was on his way to the house. Marta Young and I went over to Grant Street Inn and picked up the Fucillas and brought them back to the house so they could see Gayle." They had heard, from Gayle.

"We stayed at the house till a little after 7:00. Then Kem said, 'We need to go to the office and get started.' So Kem, Steve, and I went out here, and Connie Jackson met us. We started with the folder and the plan and the e-mails.

"What really amazed me was the amount of our people who showed up out there that night. I didn't anticipate this." That made the office area an unplanned beehive, a manifestation of general shock. "Everybody just wanted to be in the building and around other people," Pete Yonkman said.

Intra-company intimacy was loosened for one snap-judgment exception. "My private line at the office was ringing off the hook," Aimee said. "At first I was a little rattled by it, and I wasn't picking it up. Then I did once, and it was a young [Bloomington] *Herald-Times* reporter, Chris Fyall—he had been out before to interview Bill. He said, 'Aimee, are *you* OK?' He was genuinely concerned. Then he said, 'I'd like to come out to the office and portray this as Bill would want it portrayed.' At first, I was reluctant, but then I thought, 'He's right. Let's do this the right way.' So he came over, interviewed some of us, took some pictures—very nice young man, very respectful. I was glad I picked up the phone and said OK. I think he caught more of the personal things." Among them, from Fyall's next-day story:

"He was an entrepreneur in the purest sense: He wanted to make something that would last," said Tom Osborne, one of the first people ever hired by Cook, and now the company's senior vice president of intellectual property development. "He did."

"Bill never changed," Steve Ferguson said. "Success never changed him, money never changed him.

"He was [always] the same person I met in 1963, when neither one of us had anything."

Kem Hawkins, president of Cook Group, said he believes Cook's legacy will be that "he knew the ultimate gift is to give and not receive—to not even think about receiving or care about receiving.

"Bill Cook lived a life that was a relentless pursuit to solve problems—to consult with physicians and colleagues on diseases or conditions that were often a death sentence and then to set out to find a cure."

"We were there pretty late Friday night, just with our e-mails," Aimee says. "We were back early Saturday morning. We finished everything at the office on Saturday, did the essential things [at the Centrum dedication] Saturday night, and decided we were all taking Sunday off from it because it was so emotional."

Five

No Chance for Privacy

At a time when they would have preferred privacy, to spend some time together helping each other through a great personal and shared loss, the fame of great wealth and prominence exacted another price on Bill Cook's family, and the circle around him. While grieving his death, they had to be on display, as a public responsibility, and they did so, reluctantly but dutifully.

"Even though he was sick, it wasn't expected, so it *was* a shock," Carl Cook said. "The hardest thing on me was we had to plan visitation, the funeral, the Celebration of Life, all the things that went with that. I didn't come in to the office for a month. I stayed home."

Looking back, Aimee Hawkins-Mungle recognizes clues that perhaps Bill Cook knew death was close. "That Thursday morning, before they put him in the hospital, he had called me, wanted me to find Larry Rink—he was having very bad chest pains and he was barely able to talk to me. One thing he said was, 'Buddy, I'm tired.'"

Then at the hospital, as the hours wound down and out-of-towners began arriving for the big event at Old Centrum, he wasn't at all the hyperactive, ultra-involved Bill Cook. "We had all these people coming, for Centrum," Aimee recalls, "and there were still some decisions to be made—they were pushing right to the very end on getting it ready. But when I'd call out there on one of those things, all of my conversations were with Gayle. He wasn't 'Oh, no, absolutely not, give me that phone!' He was just allowing it to happen."

Steve Ferguson thinks "he knew it that whole week. People around him . . . *we* didn't want to admit it. When it was going to happen was another story. That last week, I hated not to see him every day. I wasn't surprised at all."

"The amazing thing is he really didn't complain about it," Kem Hawkins said. "I remember one day he leaned on the counter outside his office and said, 'You know, I just don't know that it's worth it.' But it was so rare that he ever complained. He did everything he could to come in, to have that continual work ethic, and to find other things to do rather than complain."

It was Bill's abrupt departure from Bloomington Hospital that last morning that "makes me wonder," Larry Rink said. "Maybe he did have a premonition this was it."

Gayle Cook's observations carry considerable weight with Rink. "Every time I was at the house talking with Bill, Gayle was always there, listening, taking it in," he said. "Bill knew he wasn't doing well, he knew he was going to die—but he could sit there and show you the boat he was building, like he was going to live another 20 years. I've always heard, 'Prepare for the worst but plan for the best.' He really did that."

ONE DAY, TWO MEMORIES

George Ridgway did a lot of remembering that morose weekend. About the time that he heard the news. The circumstances. The call that brought him the news.

"I had been over to Canton that day," he said. Since the beginning of work on the Randolph Building, a Cook airplane had taken six or more people from Bloomington to Canton at least every other Friday to check on things. "I just came in the door at home when I got the call from Aimee." It was stunning news. That suddenly, he had lost his best friend. And of course there were tears. "It was very emotional," he said.

In the next few hours and days, two stories in particular came back to George Ridgway and produced a smile, as they have ever since. Both happened "the day Bill wanted to fly my airplane down at Cedar Farm [the Cooks' weekend getaway home, a preserved antebellum estate on the Ohio River]," he says.

"It was Thanksgiving. He invited my wife and me down there. I flew my Dakota down. When I lined up to land on his grass runway, I thought, 'It's a little narrower than I remember.' When I got out I paced it off and they *had* narrowed it—42 feet, from corn row to corn row. And the wing span on that airplane was 36. I had three feet on each side."

Ridgway said Cook picked them up in a golf cart, and on the ride from the airplane to the house, leaned over and said:

"George, I have an itch."

"What is it?"

"To fly your airplane."

"Uhhh, you wouldn't mind if I went with you, would you?"

"No, that'd be fine! Let's go!"

Ridgway can't repress a smile as he continues. "I talked him into going ahead and eating the meal, hoping that he would forget. We ate—Gayle had fixed apple pie, and as soon as his fork hit the plate after his last bite of pie, he said, 'Let's go fly!' He didn't forget.

"We got it fired up, taxied to the end of the runway, did a run-up to make sure everything was working, and off we go.

"He did a great job of flying—light plane, he had flown the jets, flown the Conquest, great pilot. He did an excellent job for having no time in my plane whatsoever, till that day. There's what you call a coordinated pilot. The ball's in the center, the wings are level; you go into a turn, the ball is in the center, the wings are askew. That means you're coordinated: you're not skidding through the air, you're not slipping through the air. All the stuff he did that day, the ball was in the center, all the time. He still had the touch.

"We fly to the Brandenburg Bridge over the Ohio River and turn east over Brandenburg, Kentucky, heading toward Fort Knox [besides a military base, primary site for the U.S. gold reserve]. My GPS starts flashing a yellow light— 'Restricted Air Space 10 miles ahead.' For Fort Knox.

"I said, 'We need to peel off here.' He keeps flying straight toward Fort Knox. Then the GPS starts flashing red. He said, 'What's happening?' I said, 'Now, they're interrogating us, through the transponder, and they know who we are.'

"He smiled and said, 'They know who *you* are.'"

Cook did peel off "and flew toward Corydon, Indiana," Ridgway said. "Then he started giving me all the air speeds, flap speeds, landing air speeds, all that. I knew what was coming: he was going to put that plane on the ground."

Land it, back home at Cedar Farm.

"So, he brings it around and lines it up. There's a bit of a crosswind and he's not using enough rudder, so I start pushing a little bit on the right rudder. '*I'm* flying this airplane! Get your *foot* off the rudder!' I told him I was just resting my foot. He knew better.

"We're starting to do the landing, he's got it set up good, but he's not hold-ing enough right rudder, so the plane scoots over the top of the corn and he took it back up. Second approach, same thing's happening. We go back up. This time he said:

"'Oh, *here,* you take it. I'm afraid I'm going to hurt my corn.'"

Ridgway landed the plane and walked away with a very personal, very private treasure trove:

"Within two hours, he gave me two long-lasting memories:

"They know who *you* are."

and

"You take it. I'm afraid I'm going to hurt my corn."

CANTON REACTS

The word of Bill Cook's death got to Canton quickly, first of all to Bill and Ellie Carper, way up high on that closest-to-Bill list of his close friends since high school. Their role was to pass it on among what Gayle Cook calls "that bunch of boys who were all photographed together in their senior robes" in Canton High's Class of '49: Gus Elliott, John Myers, Pete Laken, Bob Lind-bloom, Ron Casson, Fred Mercer, Len Kuchen, and Jim Van Sickle. Those eleven, with their spouses, some of the girls in the class and their spouses, and a few friends from classes just before or after, stayed close as the decades rolled by. It was a remarkable bond that was helped by what Gayle called "unique circumstances" that kept most of them in or near Canton. That close-ness, that group "kept Bill going back," she said.

Amused by the increased celebrity that came to them as their association with the new community hero got around, a couple of years earlier the group had let him know his own special standing with them. Using the occasion of their 60th class reunion in 2009, they declared both the pride and fondness they all felt regarding the class' most noted member, and the appreciation they and all Canton felt toward him. The Canton *Ledger* printed the text of their presentation to the Cooks that night:

"Generous Heart" Award from Canton Class of '49

The Canton High School Class of 1949—on the 60th anniversary of its graduation—wishes to recognize class member Bill Cook for his generous heart, related to his hometown of Canton, Illinois, for the following reasons:

Bill Cook has always stayed in touch with his high-school friends.

Bill Cook has always had an interest in his home town.

Bill Cook has currently under construction a medical-instrument manufacturing plant to employ several hundred workers.

Bill Cook has restored downtown buildings to return Canton's business district to its former glory and to provide desirable housing.

Bill Cook has purchased other sites for construction and aesthetic improvements.

Because Bill Cook has believed that Canton gave him "roots and wings" and is now giving them back to us to move our hometown forward, we wish to acknowledge the special man he is.

Therefore, the Canton High School Class of 1949, supported by the residents of our area, commends Bill Cook, his family, and his company with this Generous Heart Award.

Thank you, Bill and Gayle.

The *Ledger* story said 99 people attended the reunion, including 60 members of the class and 39 spouses. The Cooks, of course, were two of the 99.

"BILL LOVED CANTON"

George Ridgway was the one who called Canton Mayor Kevin Meade, who was on a business trip having dinner at a restaurant. "It hit me hard," Meade said. "I remember two things he said. One was the way he started, 'Kevin, I've lost my best friend.' And the other thing he said to me—and I always knew it: 'Kevin, Bill loved Canton.'

"George asked me not to say anything to anybody until they got things straightened out over there. I went back and finished dinner. I went back to the hotel, got online, and the word was out. Once I saw that, I called my wife, and I called Chrissie."

The city attorney also was dining at a restaurant. "At first, I couldn't understand Kevin," Chrissie Peterson says. "Then I realized he was crying. My first thought was something had happened to his wife or his girls. So I stepped outside. He told me Bill had passed away.

"I was devastated, most devastated for Kevin, because I could tell it was like his Joe DiMaggio was gone. He so respected him in business and in life. He was heartbroken."

When artists Scott and Tracy Snowman heard, their thoughts got very personal. "We had gone over to West Baden . . . at Thanksgiving . . . and he was there," Scott said. Tracy said: "We had decided instead of Christmas gifts that year we were going to treat ourselves to a West Baden trip. Three days—two at West Baden, one at French Lick. We wanted to see the lighting of the Christmas tree. The St. Benedictine Sisters were there, too. We got a balcony room, we got massages, we really treated ourselves.

"And there *he* was—he came out of the dining room with Gayle and Carl and Marcy and the baby. There's something very sweet about a man with a baby. To see him with that baby girl, that was priceless."

Scott said, "At the lighting of the tree, he kept coming over to us. We went back up to the balcony and he was still there for another hour, getting his picture taken, talking to anybody who would come up to talk to him."

"That was the last time we saw him," Tracy said.

The Show Goes On

On the north side of Indianapolis, grief had arrived late on Friday with a companion: momentary panic. What *is* the right thing to do at the Centrum . . . tomorrow?

"I was coming back from getting a haircut when I got the call," Marsh Davis says.

"We were living in fear that something was going to go wrong—the sprinklers would go off, something. But nothing like that. When he and Gayle were at that wedding, Bill looked terrific.

"We had a committee for this event—we called it the Wondrous Opening Weekend—WOW. First thing in the morning on Saturday, we got together, sat around a table. We discussed everything from 'Do we pull the plug on this event?' to 'What *do* we do?'

"We realized Bill wouldn't have wanted to pull the plug."

Gayle Cook remembered, "Bill had said, 'No matter what happens to me, that event goes on.' He told me that."

Of course Davis reached out to Gayle and Carl Cook by phone, for condolences. And the secondary topic couldn't be avoided. "They were basically telling us, 'We want to handle this the best way, but we're not sure what that is,'" Carl recalls. "Mom and I both said, 'You've been planning this thing for months. There's no way you can postpone it. Just go ahead and do it.'

"And I think that is what Dad would have wanted: 'Go ahead and have it and have fun with it.'

"I don't think there's anybody who thought that was the wrong decision. I don't think it would have helped anything to have postponed it. They were unsure, but just the logistics of trying to postpone something like that. . . ."

Even going ahead was not simple. As Davis had said weeks before, the place had to be ready for opening night because the first turnout was going to pack the place. But would it? Every person, every couple planning to be there surely had the same consternation: "They *will* postpone this . . . won't they?" Word got out loosely that the dedication was going on, but in several hundred minds the same questions jangled:

"Is this . . . right?"

"*Should* we go?"

The same answer apparently came to every wonderer, because when it was time to start the dedication program, every seat was filled. And every mind wondered: Where do we go from here?

Davis was the master of ceremonies. Davis had the answer. He didn't feel compelled to say anything on-stage about what had happened. Who hadn't heard the news? He immediately acknowledged that the proper opening would be a moment of silence out of respect for the passing of . . . But that's not where he went. Silence, he said, would not honor Bill Cook, would not *be* Bill Cook.

Going ahead with the program, rather than postponing it, had been the consensus "at our WOW committee meeting that Saturday morning," Davis confided later. "So then it was, 'How do we make this something less than really somber?' At that time, I proposed, 'What if instead of a moment of silence we had a moment of noise?'

"One of the people said, 'Oh, don't do that! Nobody would understand it.'

"I said, 'I'm going to do it.'"

And he did. He urged everyone in the audience to remember the brass-loving Bill Cook and raise the roof with a moment of pure, raucous noise.

And it happened.

Just that quickly the tension of the program broke. Smiles came out. And, oh, for a good minute, it was loud and clamorous and . . .

Perfect.

For the most imperfect of happenstances.

Cook Group president Kem Hawkins marveled. "A stroke of brilliance," he called it. "A cloud was really hanging low. And everyone in there who knew Bill knew that was exactly the way he would have wanted that handled."

Aimee Hawkins-Mungle said, "We were just all in such a daze by the time we got there—so foggy. He couldn't have done anything better."

"It broke the tension," said Gayle Cook, who of course was not there. "They wanted to acknowledge Bill somehow but not make it a downer. I was very pleased that Marsh was able to do that."

Carl *was* there, a decision he made "at kind of the last minute. There was no way I was going to go up there for the whole thing—sit there and eat dinner. I didn't want it to turn into a huge receiving line."

His decision really had less to do with the dedication or honoring the building than with representing his father in a role the whole Cook family valued. The Indiana Landmarks' award (in essence, the Indiana Historic Preservationist of the Year) had been given first to, and formally named for, Bill, Gayle, and Carl Cook for the "Save of the Century" with the West Baden and French Lick Hotels. This was to be the first subsequent presentation of the Cook Cup to someone else. The recipient was a close family friend, Richard Ford of Wabash. The cited reason for his 2011 selection was a fitting link with the Cup's origin: Ford led the Cook-style preservation effort that had converted a decaying 90-year-old one-time downtown Wabash hotel building into the beautiful Charley Creek Inn, complete with a restaurant, cocktail lounge with piano bar, retail stores at street level, and a party room on the roof.

"I just really wanted to say a few words," Carl said. "I was looking forward to presenting the Cook Cup to Richard. He is one of the people I really, really admire. I have virtually unlimited respect for him, and this award I knew was something that meant a lot to him.

"I just decided I would go up there, give him the Cup, say a few words, and then I would get out of there—and that's exactly what I did."

Gayle Cook endorsed every aspect of all that. "He didn't want to short-change Richard Ford, getting this award. And he told Marsh Davis not to make it a downer, that all these people had paid lots of money, a lot didn't even know Bill, go ahead and do what you can. There was no way to say, 'OK, let's do this program next week.' It was best, and we were very pleased."

As one of the dedication program highlights, John Mellencamp, the only known Rock 'n' Roll Hall of Famer who once had a billionaire for his band's bus driver, turned down his guitar amplifier for a sentimental tribute to that bus driver. He softly sang "Save Some Time to Dream"—"a *very* nice touch" Davis said.

Save some time to dream
Save some time for yourself
Don't let your time slip away
Or be stolen by somebody else

Save some time for those you love
For they'll remember what you gave
Save some time for the songs you sing
And the music that you make

Save some time for sorrow
'Cause it's surely gonna come your way
And prepare yourself for failure
It'll give you strength some day

Could it be that this is all there is?
Could it be there's nothing more at all?
Save some time to dream
'Cause your dream might save us all

Mellencamp's sheer presence was "another thing about that day," Davis noted. "I thought, 'If Bill's not here, John's not going to show up.' Bill was the one who got him for us, and he's probably the only one who could have. But John did come, and the two songs he picked were perfect ["Longest Days" was the other]—and he was sick, from the flu."

There was even more to his appearance than that. Including Mellencamp in the dedication program began as a "wouldn't it be great if" kind of whimsy among the planners, none among them bold enough even to make a call asking. But Cook heard about it, said "I'll call him," did, and got an instant commitment. "But when the time came around," Davis says, "John had forgotten to put down the date he had agreed to with Bill—just totally forgot it. He was booked to play in Edmonton, Canada, that same day." That problem surfaced just a matter of days ahead of the date, which—on Bill Cook Time—turned out to be ample.

"We went to work with Bill and his aviation people," Davis said. "Edmonton is two hours behind us. We rearranged our whole program to start really early. Mellencamp would do his short set here, then we'd whisk him off to the airport and one of the Cook jets would get him to Edmonton. They delayed their program an hour—and it all worked."

Seven

A Day of Remembering

For Dr. Larry Rink, the time from hearing about Bill Cook's death while in China to getting to Bloomington is a blur. "I got back the next day," he says. "I didn't go home. I went right to the house. I can't believe I wasn't around."

It has been more than two years now, and that knowingly irrational feeling hasn't passed. Since another of his close friends, basketball coach Bob Knight, was the U.S. Olympic coach in 1984, Rink has been involved with international sports physicians' groups and risen to the highest ranking possible. The business card he was given by the International University Sports Federation identifies him as "Chair Medical Committee."

Within the field, doctors can serve at just one Olympics, and Rink's time came at Barcelona in 1992. But, just as big in scope and number of participating countries and athletes is the every-two-years International University Games, and that is the group he continued to serve up through the summer 2013 edition in Kazan, Russia.

In April 2011, three months ahead of that biennial's games in Shenzhen, China, Rink was at the booming city of ten million just north of Hong Kong to meet with the international heads of delegations for a final review of preparations. "I talked to them about doping control and medical care and issues like that for them to take back and tell their medical people. It was the last meeting before competition. You take them out and show the facilities. We do that in the Olympics. I had made it as short a trip as I could make it, partially because of Bill. I knew how sick he was. That was a two-day meeting. I worked it out where I'd only be gone four and a half days."

It was the wrong four and a half days.

"I got a phone call. Early morning." There's a twelve-hour time difference between Bloomington and Shenzhen. At about 5:00 in the morning Saturday, April 16, 2011, Dr. Larry Rink learned that the long, long fight he and his friend had fought was over.

"I just was . . . I was devastated. Obviously everybody around him knew it was going to happen sometime. But I felt . . . *incredibly* guilty. He left town at times, and I left town at times, but . . . it didn't seem right. Not that I think I could have saved him. It just seemed . . . we had a deal, so to speak—an unwritten kind of thing . . . that we would know the time and, just . . . maybe let it happen.

"But I have to admit . . . I felt like I let Gayle down. I still do."

There had been some very narrow escapes those last ten or twelve years, escapes that came back to Larry Rink with a myriad of other joys and fears, triumphs and traumas as he was flying back from China.

Maybe the closest of the close calls, certainly a turning point, came when the Cooks were on a New Year's outing in London as 1998 began and a heart attack sent Bill to a holiday-understaffed hospital. The combination of the attack's severity and the, perhaps, sub-normal immediate treatment, caused major irreparable damage. Rink flew over in a specially equipped plane to bring him back for testing and treatment in Bloomington. Going over, even after seeing him there, Rink says, "I thought he would survive. I'm an optimist. What I didn't know till he got back was how much damage he had. When I found that out [through tests], that's when I called Gayle in and told them both to get their affairs in order. But he lived a long time after that."

In 2002, an evening attack that Cook himself thought to be a muscle problem, maybe a kidney stone flare-up, turned out to be irreparable renal failure. "That was another major problem in taking care of him," Rink said. "When your kidneys don't work right and your heart doesn't work right—that's a bad combination. A lot of the medicines to treat heart failure can lessen your kidney function. Every time we tried to use the most common medicines for this, his kidney function would deteriorate. So we used nitroglycerine with him." About four years later, Rink says, a medical journal article told of someone else's stumbling onto trying "nitro" in a kidney crisis and finding, "Hey, this works pretty well."

Another feeling of "this could be it" came for Rink in 2009 when Cook made his last Cleveland Clinic trip to have fluid drawn off. "He seemed to be on a spiraling downward course," Rink said. "His kidney function had gotten worse. We weren't making headway on the fluid. I was hoping he'd go up there and they'd come up with something, because they see the sickest and the worst of everything. The people up there basically told me 'We don't have anything to offer.' I was disappointed."

There was so little in medical history to offer guidance or hope.

"I could probably count on one hand other patients I have had who had to have the [paracentesis] procedure," Rink said. Even fewer fingers were needed to count the ones who survived more than a few such treatments. "For him to do that for two years—it was really incredible.

"Both of us kept hoping that something would come along. We talked a lot about a heart transplant. He didn't want a transplant. He wanted to wait for stem-cell research to become clinical."

But Rink had his own thoughts, highly personal where this one man was concerned, this one man whose fortune had been amassed in the continuing process of saving lives.

"We talked to people at Mass General, at Northwestern, Cleveland Clinic, obviously Indianapolis—no one would even consider him for a heart transplant. That really frustrated me. I realize he was 80, he had bad vascular disease, he had several things—he falls out on age, on kidney disease, and falls out on every vascular disease. He had a carotid artery operated on, he had to have an artery in his kidney dilated once—every vessel of that size in his body, which are basically kidney, legs, heart, and brain, he had disease in all of them—not just disease but disease enough to cause symptoms. He had what we call claudication, that's when you walk with pain in your legs.

"But it seems to me that sometimes, when you're dealing with *great* people . . . you break the mold. I think a transplant would have extended his life another five or ten years because I really do believe we had been able to stop the progression of his vascular disease. After London he didn't have another actual heart attack. He had his carotid artery bypassed and we studied it with Dopler studies [ultrasound tests of blood flow] and that hadn't progressed."

Rink did win one battle against medical preferences—and one battle of wills with Bill Cook. He finally did get a defibrillator inserted.

"Bill did not fit all the qualifications to get a defibrillator, because people with this problem usually die one of two ways: from heart failure, when your heart just wears out or just can't sustain blood pressure to the organs any more, or electrical death, where your heart goes into a bizarre rhythm, and that can be prevented—it's a shame for *anybody* to die from that. It took us at least two years to convince Bill to put a defibrillator in, but any even casual conversation he had with a cardiologist—and I suspect he had several that I don't know about—I'm sure they all told him, 'You need a defibrillator.'"

The thought triggered another Rink smile, because even within his own patients, Bill Cook wasn't alone in that stubbornness about accepting a defibrillator. "I had two patients who were really reluctant to have that done. Herman Wells was the other one." Some pair. Wells, the 25-year president of Indiana University, whose impact on the university and the state started in the 1930s and carried to his death in the 2000s, was a giant in Bill Cook's eyes, a man he admired to the point of revering, and on his end Wells clearly enjoyed his relationship with Cook the man and Cook the company.

Both men eventually gave in and had a defibrillator implanted, their reasons for reluctance slightly different, Rink says. "Herman would say, 'I've lived long enough. Let's save that for someone younger.' Bill was afraid it might keep him alive but as a vegetable. Herman's went in ten years before he died. Bill's was put in in April 2009, so he had it two years. But it took at least two years to get him to do it. He could be stubborn. I think he honestly believed it would not help him. But I think it did. If your heart gets into a bizarre rhythm, the defibrillator detects the problem, and shocks you and gets you out of it. To my knowledge Bill's never fired. We would check it. That tells me even more that at the end his heart just wore out."

Dr. John Strobel, the last doctor who attended Cook and established his time of death, was the cardiologist who implanted Bill Cook's defibrillator. A Shelbyville native, an Indiana University undergraduate and Medical School graduate, Strobel is an electro-physiologist, a partner with Rink in practice at Bloomington since the early 2000s. "He's not nationally known, but in my opinion he's that good," Rink says. "He's state president of the American College of Cardiologists." Within the office, some have called him "Larry Rink Jr.," as a compliment to both.

In the Bill Cook-Larry Rink relationship, the doctor certainly didn't do all the talking or the patient all the listening. "Bill taught me a lot of things,"

Rink said. "I had always been a proponent of exercise, but he taught me the real value of it. Exercise was key to him.

"And he taught me that feeling bad . . . part of that really *is* a state of mind. There's no way he could have felt well the last couple of years he lived. No way. But I think you can be so damned strong you can almost get by that."

To the end, Rink felt Bill Cook never conceded that the impossible couldn't happen: that someday, somehow, with some scientific breakthrough, he might beat that congestive heart yet.

"Every time we did blood tests, he and I would just hang on every piece of information we had," Rink said. "If I did a blood test and I didn't get back to him within two hours, either he was calling or Aimee was calling, just to see how his kidney functioning responded.

"The last three years his blood pressure was always in the low range—90 to 100. I told him once: 'Bill, your best blood pressure is as low as you can get it, stand up, and not pass out.' We were always pushing the envelope with anything we did with him. When he was admitted the last time, the number was below 90. But he would walk around a lot with blood pressures of 88 to 90 to 92 when most people wouldn't, and he'd look pretty darned good.

"We would celebrate minor improvements—a milestone! Quite frankly, it probably didn't mean much, but *we* believed it—we were all hoping.

"He understood a lot about physiology. Sometimes it got him in trouble—two and two seemed to equal four but it didn't always. I'm sure I never did everything perfectly with him, either. A lot of what we did with him his last few years was almost experimenting.

"He would try to bargain about some things with medicine. I found a note he signed 'Bill at home.' He was having a problem, and he said, 'I think it's due to this medicine, so I'm going to stop this medicine. Is it ok with you?' I wrote back, 'That's not the cause of your problem, and, *yes,* I do care.'

"So I was always having to check his medicines. Every two or three months, I would call the pharmacist at Cook Clinic. I knew what he was supposed to take, but I didn't always know what he *was* taking. Bill knew. He'd have his list at home and 'correct' it.

"But the last three years he lived, he took meticulous care of himself. And I suspect Gayle was right in there watching with him. Because no average person could have lived with what he had."

And not just lived—rebuilt towns and buildings.

"Just think about this: every week he'd go into that hospital, early in the morning, lie there, get tubes put in, go through all that—then he'd nap, get up, and go back to the office—without even going home sometimes," Rink said.

"And he never complained."

Rink broke off from somber memories into a smile. "Well, I can't say never. He did complain about how much the albumin cost. He was even looking online trying to find other companies that maybe made this stuff cheaper.

"I will say this: his last two years it took an army to keep him going.

"But there was no question he was the general."

Eight

Just the Silence

That first day back at work, the Monday that ended the weekend that began with Bill Cook's death, is not a forgotten day, probably throughout the Cook Group empire but certainly in the Park 48 headquarters of the company. Most remembered is the quiet of the day—not so much in gloom, more in what came across as a determined, unified resolve that things would go on as Bill Cook would have wanted, that his high performance standards would be continued, that the company he had conceived, built and nurtured would, indeed, not drop off an iota in keeping the customer, the product buyer, the trusting, vulnerable patient uppermost in mind.

Everyone in the building that day, and the next one or two or three, would have his or her own memory, own interpretation. "I think people had their heads down and were working, and didn't want to laugh, because it would have been almost sacrilegious, almost an insult at that time," Kem Hawkins says.

It was the troupers' tribute: the show must go on.

"My memories of that day are . . . just the silence," Aimee Hawkins-Mungle says. "And the outpouring of individuals who wanted to come up here [to the second-floor executive office area that included Bill Cook's office].

"We certainly allowed it. I just thought, 'If that's what they need, I'm happy to stand out here all day long.' And that's kind of what we did. We just touched employees that day.

"It was amazing to me—the concern they had, not for themselves, but the fact that Bill was gone. It wasn't, 'Oh my gosh, what does this mean for me? Are you closing the doors?' They wanted to know what happened. They wanted to know how Gayle was."

The Friday afternoon timing that had dictated its own release date on news of the surprise death did come up on Monday, Aimee said. "A few older employees told me, 'I was devastated when I picked up the paper Saturday.' That's how they found out. All I could say was, 'I'm so sorry.' Unfortunately, with our size, it was unavoidable. We did the best we could."

Following the plan drawn up Friday night and Saturday, she said, "We had manager and supervisor meetings first thing Monday morning—eight o'clock, about 250 supervisors and managers who came in from each of the different plants—to be sure they understood what had happened, and what was going to happen. You could have heard a pin drop in that room. Completely silent."

Company president Kem Hawkins was the principal speaker in the short managers' meeting, and executive vice president Pete Yonkman said, "Kem did a masterful job. I think those people were waiting for direction—how were we going to handle this? It felt very heavy. They didn't know how to act." Hawkins shifted the managers' feelings to their role, Yonkman says. "Kem just told them, 'We need to give everybody a sense of, it's going to be OK. Nothing is going to change. We're going to mourn his loss and then we're going to do what he wanted us to do.'

"That message got out, through a variety of ways—e-mails and phone calls and memos and management meetings, all sorts of things."

Aimee Hawkins-Mungle said, "We didn't do anything over the loudspeaker. And immediately I started a huge condolence box, because cards started flooding in here for Gayle—people just wanted to tell her how sorry they were. We took several loads to her, which I thought was a wonderful, wonderful thing . . . until I realized, being Gayle Cook, she wanted to answer every single one! I went over to the house and in the living room there were piles: Employees, Friends, Family . . . I said, 'What *is* all this?' She said, 'I have to answer these.' I said, 'Oh, no, no, no, absolutely not!' But, she went through every single one of them, and some things we pulled out and put in books and binders. It was . . . remarkable. And her reaction to it was remarkable, too—'I need to touch every one of these people.'"

Bill Cook's beloved 1950 Studebaker had a
place of honor in front of Cook Headquarters
when people came to pay their respects.

Nine

A Day at the Office

Saturday, April 23, the eighth day after Bill Cook's death, was set for a public tribute at Park 48, the George Ridgway-conceived "horizontal skyscraper" on Bloomington's western outskirts. The handsome Cook World Headquarters building represents the full flowering of the manufacturing idea that started in an unused apartment bedroom. It's a building with a grand fountain out front, its expanse outward, not up. The effect so impressive that even Bill Cook once admitted that, not every day but now and then, approaching the building, he would look straight ahead through his windshield at fountain and flags and building and "get a kind of awe—gee whiz!"

At ten o'clock on an appropriately gray and gloomy Saturday morning, the building was opened for people to come and pay their respects—and that, openly and affectionately, is precisely what they did, long lines of them.

The public tribute had begun Friday in the downtown where Bill and Gayle Cook had such a pronounced and lasting effect. The "Canopy of Lights," which lights up the courthouse square each Christmas season, went up and came on in the middle of spring, in twinkling recognition of the man who for his last 25 years had helped make the lighting even brighter.

It's a tradition that continues. Jim Murphy, whose role as head of CFC Properties includes overseeing the annual lighting, laughs as he remembers the one time he and Bill Cook talked dollars on that matter. "Several years ago I thought, 'I'm going to let Bill know how much he spends on decorations at Christmas time each year.' So I did some checking, and it is about $50,000 a year, including the lights and the labor by Cook employees to put them up.

After a last lap around his favorite spots, Bill Cook's cortege arrives.

Originally we wrapped the trees with lights like you do typically at home, but a few years ago Steve Ferguson had been up to Chicago and seen how they wrap every branch, and he said, 'This year I want *us* to wrap every branch.' So we did. There's like 280,000 lights, 28 miles in length.

"We leave them on the trees, but every three years—because naturally there's damage: trucks run into them, things like that—we take them down and put in new lights.

"One night Bill and Gayle, Steve and Connie Ferguson, and my wife Cathy and I went out to dinner. We were walking downtown and I told Bill the cost of the lights was running about $50,000 a year.

"He gave me a look and said, 'Scrooge! Bah, humbug!'"

Murphy tried to counter: "No, Bill. Christmas is my favorite holiday of the year. I just thought you might want to know how much you're spending.

"He looked at me and said: 'You know what, Murph? We're giving people something to smile about. I want to do more.'

"I didn't think about it until later, but that was the first Christmas after 9/11. And he made that statement: 'I want to give people something to smile about.'

"Isn't that beautiful?"

En route to the viewing Saturday morning, the hearse carried the Cook casket in an escorted procession through the downtown, under the lighted canopy, past most of the downtown buildings brought back to life by the Cook touch, even past IU basketball's Cook Hall, a ceremonial last swing on the way to the public tribute at Park 48. The doors opened on time, and for hours lines formed outside with people waiting to come into the crowded area. There the top people of Cook Inc. greeted them, the men wearing dark suits and ties, an appropriate but rare sight in a building where the head man himself had set a tie-less, informal dress code, defending it with wry humor: "We do *own* coats and ties. We just don't wear them here." This day they did.

From that ten o'clock opening until well after six, when the last of the callers left, Bill Cook's top people, most notably Carl and wife Marcy, were there. It was too soon for Gayle to meet the public that way. "Carl stayed there all through it. I just didn't think I could."

In the next morning's Bloomington *Herald-Times,* reporter Mike Leonard wrote:

"Hundreds lined up . . . in a light rain . . . awaiting their
opportunity" to pay last respects to Bill Cook.

The scene at the Cook Group's world headquarters Saturday looked
very much like a memorial service for a president or head of state.
Hundreds of people lined up outside the central building on Bloomington's west side under umbrellas in a light rain before the doors
were opened at 10 AM and the line was brought inside. Mourners in
suits and formal dresses mingled with people in jeans and casual
clothes, awaiting their opportunity to pass by the late William A.
Cook's flag-draped casket inside the stately rotunda.

It was the perfect cosmopolitan mix, differing from Leonard's apt "president or head of state" reference only in the way the passersby stayed inside the
building after their solemn walk past the casket and through the handshakes
of appreciation by Carl and Marcy Cook, Kem Hawkins and Steve Ferguson,
Pete Yonkman and all the people of Cook, stayed to talk among themselves,
to exchange stories, and to smile, even laugh. "You know," one of the milling
group said, "the amazing thing is that everyone in here right now feels like he
or she really knew Bill, was a *friend* of his."

"I think about my relationship with him," Yonkman said. "As people were
coming through, they all had their relationship. He had that depth of relation-

ships with, at any given time, hundreds of people—Canton, and Cedar Farm, and IU, politics—it's staggering to think of how he was able to maintain all those relationships, and the depth of them. And it was genuine. Amazing."

The man who walked with hardhat through construction areas at the West Baden and French Lick hotels, greeting foremen and workers by name, asking about their families, that was the man described; the top executive who, as Benedictine Order Sister Rose Mary Rexing once recalled, on her first visit at his office had "walked with me on my way out. We passed by some woman employees with their hair in nets, and he greeted each of them, with so much obvious respect. I could not forget that." Those were the people who didn't forget things like that, either, and came to say goodbye, as did Sister Rose Mary and a full delegation from the monastery of the Sisters of St. Benedict at Ferdinand, Indiana, not far from French Lick.

Off to the side, behind them, as Carl and Marcy met the estimated 5,000 who came through that day, were a couple of enlarged photographs, one of grandfather Bill Cook, large hand down and gripped by the tiny one of 15-month-old Eleanor, walking toward the camera but oblivious to it, and then a second of them with the same hand-in-hand link, walking away. They were pictures so very arresting, taken within a week of Bill's death by Marcy on the sidewalk in front of the Cooks' 40-plus-year home. "He had chosen to be called Granddad, and Eleanor could say that," Gayle said.

Somewhere during that period, away from the public eye, was Bill Cook's funeral. "It was a very brief service, shortly after the viewing," Gayle says. Only relatives were there, except for the Sisters of St. Benedict, who officiated. The Cooks were not Catholic, but they had developed a friendship with the Sisters from the Ferdinand monastery, helping them raise funds with events at his two hotels and golf courses, contributing to the renovation of their domed sanctuary, and assisting them in lining up the same Wisconsin firm (Conrad Schmitt) that had done the dome work at West Baden. "Sister Kristine Anne Harpenau [prioress at the monastery] and Sister Barbara Lynn Schmitz did the service," Gayle says. "They were such good ladies and friends—the nicest little family you have ever seen. Ministers could take lessons from them. It was very personal, a cluster of relatives and friends—basically, my family, Marcy's family, and Van and Judy Fucilla, on Bill's side."

Facing. A portrait, a farewell in the world headquarters of the company Bill Cook built.

CELEBRATING THE LIFE AND LEGACY

William A. Cook

June 01, 2011

Indiana University Auditorium

Reception: 5:30 pm - 6:15 pm

Celebration: 6:30 pm

en

Celebrating Quite a Life

Left was one final chance for Bloomington, Indiana University, so very many from his many interests, to say the final thank you they wanted to express.

On June 1, a month and a half after Bill Cook's death, in the stately Indiana University Auditorium late on a Wednesday afternoon, his remarkable 80-year life was duly and formally and joyfully and at times tearfully celebrated.

The program's unscheduled star was 17-month-old Eleanor, who scrambled up a formidable set of stairs and toddled on-stage as her father was speaking and praising her grandfather. It couldn't have been better scripted. In mid-talk, Carl glanced to the side to see his surprise visitor approach, greeted her with "Oh, hi, Eleanor!" and, with a smiling, one-armed swoop, picked her up. That was the charming page one picture that spotlighted the *Herald-Times* coverage of the event: child in arm as Dad spoke.

"*Totally* unplanned," Gayle Cook calls that part of a special evening. "Marcy and I were in the front row on the far right, and the steps are on the far left of the stage. Marcy had Eleanor standing in front of her. She'd wander out a little, then she'd turn around and come back—she wasn't going to leave Marcy. Then she started walking, and I thought, 'I could grab her, but if I do, she might scream.'"

Naturally, both Marcy and Gayle presumed she would take a few steps more, then turn around and come back. But . . . "She didn't turn around— she *never* turned around, she just kept walking all the way to that side of the stage," Gayle says. "We could not even see that there were steps. But she knew. She walked right over there and went up the steps—on her hands and knees,

I understand. The tape of that just shows her emerging—there's a pair of hands that helped her up, as she got to the top of the steps. I don't know how she even knew where to go, but she did. And then . . ."

"Marcy was trying to get my attention," Carl says, "but I couldn't see or hear anything up there. We didn't even know she *could* go up stairs yet.

"I didn't see her until, out of the corner of my eye, she got up the last step. She kind of slithered past the guy who was standing there, got up the stairs, and the next thing you know she's there. What are you going to do? I just picked her up and tried to figure out where I was, speaking."

He was in the midst of thanking people for their tributes to his father and adding a very high one of his own: "A lot of very nice things were said about my dad. The thing *I* will say: in my unbiased opinion, I had the best dad in the world. My mother had the best husband in the world. And my daughter had the best grandfather in the world."

Later, Carl said, "I don't know if my remarks conveyed everything I wanted to say. It was hard for me to do, just on a personal and emotional level. I was so relieved when it was over. I dreaded doing that. It was painful and I had all that time to worry about it—1½ months, it was just hanging there for me the whole time." He was the only one who had doubts. A reader said on the *Herald-Times* website: "With all the different words being tossed about describing Mr. Cook by a lot of people, I think Bill would be most proud of the heartfelt words uttered by his son, Carl, that he was a loving family man. Job well done, Carl, well said!"

The celebration was a night when IU and the state of Indiana sent out their highest officials with tributes, when musicians representative of all Bill Cook's spectrum-spanning tastes performed splendidly, and when recipients of Bill and Gayle Cook's philanthropic and hands-on support all joined in a program that was fast-moving even judged on Bill Cook time.

What the speakers said would have made him squirm a little. Distinguished as they were, none of the speakers, none of their words would have touched him more than the appearance and the performance of 27 alumni of the Star of Indiana, beneficiaries of and participants in Bill Cook's decade-long involvement in the combination of sport and art known as drum corps.

Facing. Carl Cook and Eleanor, an unplanned highlight.

Above, John Mellencamp; *below left,* Lindsey Medina; *below right,* Becky Saddlemire.

Above left, President Michael McRobbie;
above right, Carl Cook and Governor Mitch
Daniels; *below left,* Fred Keller; *below right,*
Tina Connor.

That decade started on a night when son Carl was at home with his dad watching a telecast of the national Drum Corps International finals and ended with a Bill Cook-backed unit, Star of Indiana, winning that competition in 1991. It was an unprecedented rocket ride from record-best first year to record-fastest championship. Star of Indiana veteran Becky Saddlemire, speaking for her fellow alumni onstage, said, "I speak for thousands when I say thank you, Carl, for convincing your father to sit down and watch Drum Corps. We did it right and we made Bill proud. And we were a family. We experienced more joy in one summer than many will ever experience in a lifetime." Their opening number, a mellow "When You Wish upon a Star," was "one of the first pieces he ever heard our drum corps play," she said. They closed with "Elsa's Procession to the Cathedral"—according to Saddlemire "the last thing he ever heard Star play."

Indiana University president Michael McRobbie, the master of ceremonies, called Cook "a legendary part of the state's history . . . a great champion of liberal education . . . an American genius." Dr. Fred Keller noted Cook was the first non-doctor to receive the highest individual honor given by both the American and the European interventional radiology societies because he through his company "fundamentally changed the way medicine is practiced." Keller is Cook Professor of Interventional Therapy at Oregon Health and Science University and director of the Dotter Institute, which was created with major assistance from Cook in honor of his longtime friend, associate and key early career-helper, Dr. Charles Dotter.

For the second time in just over a month, John Mellencamp honored him with a performance of "Save Some Time to Dream." And there was another special moment: Lindsey Medina, the vocalist who had so impressed Bill and Gayle Cook at the wedding they attended at Old Centrum, sang that same hymn: "The Lord's Prayer." Lindsey was the program's link to that day when, as George Ridgway said in retrospect, "Bill got to see the place the way he had envisioned it."

Governor Mitch Daniels supplied the quote that was the *Herald-Times'* next-morning headline ("This was a noble life") and in his part of the program made some news. He presented to Carl Cook, on behalf of his father, the state's Sachem Award, "the highest honor a Hoosier can receive," Daniels called it. The night of the wedding, Daniels said later, he had told Cook he would be receiving the rarely-presented award. It's not as well known, nor as frequently given, as the other governor-conferred honor, Sagamore of the

Wabash, which had been presented to Bill Cook three times, once each by governors Otis Bowen (1973), Evan Bayh (1991), and Daniels himself (2007). The Sachem, Daniels told the auditorium crowd, recognizes not just high achievement but also a life "of moral excellence . . . a strong sense of right and wrong."

Cook, Daniels said, "is now an historic preservation project for all of us. He has entered history. He is, as Lincoln, now one who belongs to the Ages. I am just a surrogate tonight for 6½ million Hoosiers and so many countless people beyond, who know that Bill Cook was one of those rare people whose like we are unlikely to see again but whose model, whose example, we can all take and learn so much from."

PART THREE

Outside the Lines, 2007–2011

Eleven

Zenith

"It's really a shame that he didn't get to see it because Bill enjoyed those years and months of designing the boat and seeing Aaron [Steenbhom] develop and learn and design and use his talents. . . . Bill got pleasure out of it, during that planning period."

—*Gayle Cook*

Previous page. Zenith—the boat that Bill Cook "just got such a pleasure out of" designing.

*T*he pace of Bill Cook restoration ideas and projects was quick and time-demanding, but as was the case all along in blending avocations like Drum Corps in with his avid pursuit of his medical-devices vocation, even those homestretch years included some diversions.

His declining health cut into the time he had envisioned for travel for him and Gayle in the boat that fulfilled a late-in-life dream—*Star 7*. Bill had to go to Australia to find a willing collaborator in design and construction, but when the boat was finished it provided him and Gayle with some of their best adventures on American inland waterways, mostly via navigable rivers as well as the Great Lakes and St. Lawrence Seaway, but also including some open-ocean time that whetted Bill's appetite for a second-generation boat that he visualized, helped to develop and build, but never quite got to ride in or pilot.

Still, the second boat—*Zenith* by name, also Australian-built—provided some special pleasures in those closing years, Gayle says.

Those were pleasures shared with Aaron Steenbhom and his wife Nicky, young Australians who joined the Cooks' life as boat pilots and who became tight family friends.

"Aaron is such a genius," Gayle said. "He and Bill used to sit around on *Star 7*, Bill would say, 'If we had to do the boat over again, I'd put this here, I'd have wanted this kind of engine . . .' Aaron is a self-educated engineer, one of those people who can do just anything. He could fix anything on *Star 7*, not just the engines but also the navigation, the electronics, the dishwasher, the computer, the TV. Bill took a lot of pride in seeing Aaron develop."

One of those developments came in ship designing, talking and dreaming with fellow visionary Bill Cook about taking his boating experience to a new level with *Zenith*. "You can see the parallel to other people Bill took in," Gayle said. "This young fellow who was in his 20s when he first came to us—to see him participate in the designing and overseeing the building of *Zenith*."

With the Steenbhoms, the Cooks had sailed on both the Atlantic and Pacific oceans in *Star 7*, but in restricted range. The new boat would be a major step up. "It's larger, and it's ocean-going." Gayle said. "Bill just got such a pleasure out of seeing all this happen. He never saw the finished product, but for the last year or so a favorite way for him to spend an evening was with Aaron, seeing him working out all of this."

The ship's name was a triumph of its own, and a bit of a teaser, too. The last gigantic new sales product of the Bill Cook era was the Zenith Flex AAA (Abdominal Aortic Aneurysm) Endovascular Graft, which revolutionized treatment of lower-body vascular problems around the globe. "Zenith" is a great word as a label for an ultimate product, a noun describing the sun's highest point, broadened into a descriptive term for the highest point of anything's or anyone's rise.

"*Zee*-nith," by pronunciation. But only in America. "The rest of the world says '*zinn*-uth,'" Gayle says. "We got used to saying 'zinn-uth' for the boat with our Australians, because that's what they said. Now I don't know which one to say." For its purpose, the name by any pronunciation was perfect, Gayle feels. "It means the height of good things. And, there are very few *Zenith* boats in the world, for some reason. There are other names used over and over, like *Serendipity.*

"It's really a shame that he didn't get to see it because Bill enjoyed those years and months of designing the boat and seeing Aaron develop and learn and design and use his talents."

Nicky was part of the project, too. "She got her captain's qualifications, too. The long-range plan was to bring it to Fort Lauderdale or to base it on the West Coast. Because of the range it could go anywhere. It was designed where if Bill had to have a doctor on board, there were facilities. If he had to continue this weekly procedure, we'd have to have the equipment. We'd have to find some doctor who would like to go to sea for a while.

"We hadn't got that far yet. His walking was limited, but the boat was built in such a way that you could have a motorized chair—more like a golf cart than a wheelchair, but narrow enough that you could go up a ramp. Because everywhere that you can dock a boat is lower than the land, you have to go up. It was designed so Bill could be comfortable on it."

The boat's future is uncertain. For all the carryovers in interests between the two, Carl does not have his father's passion for boating. So, *Zenith*, the dream boat that Bill Cook never got to see, is completed now and up for sale. Still, it served a purpose. "Bill got pleasure out of it, during that planning period," Gayle said.

That was a period that also included some other highlight adventures and experiences outside the lines connecting the preservation and restoration projects.

Twelve

Alger-ian Advice

APRIL 9, 2010

"What's important about the tapestry of time that is history isn't one event or a stream of events—no, what's important is how events should guide us and shape our actions. Be healthy, encourage free thinking, take care of your community, and let history be your guide."

—*Bill Cook*

Previous page. Gayle, Bill, Marcy, and Carl Cook
on the steps of the Supreme Court.

A line in *Ready, Fire, Aim!*, describing the Bloomington excitement when one of the city's own suddenly popped up in Forbes Magazine's annual listing of America's 400 richest people, reads: "Bill Cook: Horatio Alger of the 1980s. From Nothing to the Forbes 400."

That turned out to be more than a metaphor. In Washington, D.C., on April 9, 2010, 111 years after the death of nineteenth-century writer Horatio Alger Jr., the national Horatio Alger Association honored Bill and ten other great success stories at its annual awards program, a star-spangled black-tie event in Constitution Hall.

Horatio Alger is a rare name with its own connotation. The author's fiction followed a consistent "rags to riches" theme, down-and-out boys achieving the American Dream of wealth and success through hard work, courage, determination, and concern for others.

The Washington-based association that does its nationwide work in Alger's name focuses on both self-made success and the rags-to-riches part. For 63 years now, the award has spotlighted "role models for American youth [who] have triumphed over adversity and achieved professional accomplishment." Its honorees "must demonstrate loyalty and devotion to American ideals and to the American free enterprise system . . . be dedicated community leaders . . . [and] show a strong commitment to assisting those who are less fortunate in society." If there was a surprise in Bill Cook's selection it was that it didn't happen 10, 20, or 30 years earlier, or as soon as their successes from a $1,500 investment had reached the point where Bill and Gayle Cook could begin their beneficial impact on the citizenry and life around them.

Some of Cook's fellow 2010 honorees had national and international renown; most didn't. Former Secretary of State Condoleezza Rice and retired General Tommy Franks headed the list of those who did. Cook was the one of the eleven whose success had come primarily in manufacturing a product and building it to worldwide sales. In addition, Supreme Court Justice Clarence Thomas, a 1992 Alger Association honoree, received the organization's annual Norman Vincent Peale Award. Two days before, in a ceremony at the Supreme Court, Justice Thomas had presented the eleven with their Horatio Alger medallions. Rice was the keynote speaker at the group's luncheon at noon on April 9 in the Diplomatic Reception rooms at the U.S. Department of State.

The climax of the weekend of events honoring the eleven was a dinner attended by 1,200 people (including a sizable bloc of Cook employees and friends, among them Indiana University president Michael McRobbie and wife Laurie, and singer John Mellencamp). At the dinner, Cook directed his comments at more than 100 young Horatio Alger scholars, brought in from high schools around the nation, each of them with his or her own story of growing up in a difficult environment, and an achievement record that showed they were their own Horatio Alger-style success tales. Horatio himself would have loved what life and reality have done with his theme, in the life stories—fact, not fiction—that were told in the separate introductions and personal comments. Those were what Gayle Cook took home as her primary memories of the D.C. party, the "incredible accomplishments by those young scholarship recipients, from homeless orphans out on the street to college successes." Spotlighting those spectacular young achievers, assuring their education, and continuing the program for their successors came through funds raised by the Society from the primary honorees, a give-back opportunity that Cook and his fellow recipients each noted and clearly appreciated.

"Tonight we gather to honor Americans who are self-made success stories," Bill Cook told the young honorees in his time at the podium. "This is no big revelation but I've always thought that while many are successful, few are truly self-made. Successful people have this in common: they take care of their families, their friends, their colleagues, their companies, and their communities. In turn, their families, friends, colleagues, companies, and their communities take care of them.

"I've done some traveling in my time. I became a pilot not too long after I learned how to drive a car, and my experiences around the globe lead me to believe that what sets Americans apart from the rest of the world is how we think. We are free thinkers, and free thinking brings limitless opportunities, so be open to opportunity."

He had one other "suggestion" to them, as "young leaders who are here to learn something about success and achievement":

...while many
are successful,
few are truly
self-made.

Horatio Alger Society photo.

Don't be a slave to history but instead use history as a guide to
future action. What's important about the tapestry of time that is
history isn't one event or a stream of events. No, what's important
is how events should guide us and shape our actions. Let history
be your guide to future action . . . take care of yourselves. Success,
free-thinking, family and friends are important but good health is
also important. Be healthy, encourage free thinking, take care of
your community and let history be your guide.

A three-generation celebration:
Gayle, Eleanor, Bill, Marcy, and Carl Cook.

At Canton High graduation in 1948. From left, first row, Gus Elliott, John Myers,
Pete Laken, Bob Lindbloom; standing, Ron Casson, Bill Carper, Fred Mercer,
Bill Cook, Len Kuchen, Jim Van Sickle.

Sixty-two years later. Reunited at Bill Cook's Horatio Alger dinner.
From left, Len Kuchen, Jim Van Sickle, Bob Heppenstall,
Gus Elliott, Bill Carper, Bill Cook, Gene Taylor, and John Myers.

Carl, Bill, and Gayle Cook with
Horatio Alger's bust.

Facing. Bill Cook, Steve Ferguson, and Gayle Cook
with the U.S. Capitol in the background.

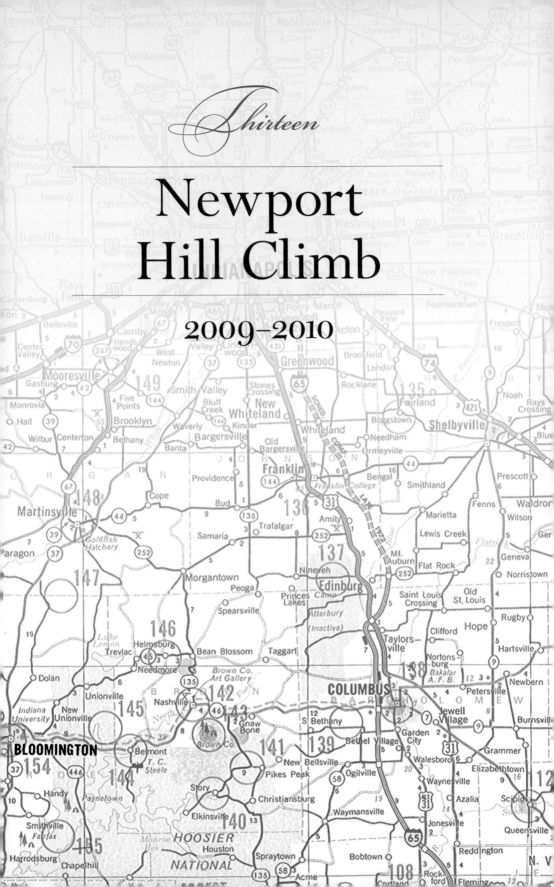

Thirteen

Newport
Hill Climb

2009–2010

"I didn't know you *could* smoke the tires with a little Studebaker like that. But he did!"

—*Carl Cook*

*N*o single word could describe Bill Cook, but competitive is one that would have to be high on any such list. That never left him, that football captain mentality that came, saw, and conquered Drum Corps, that never saw a relic revival it couldn't handle or an industrial giant too big to take on. There's a little plaque on the wall of a little building in a little town that only a few in Indiana know about that says big things about Bill Cook's competitiveness.

If you've never heard of the Newport Hill Climb, you're one of a vast majority that has a few hundred thousand exceptions, who—by shaky, unverifiable but quite believable count—make it the second-biggest annual sports event in Indiana every year, ranked by numbers of spectators. In the state that for more than 100 years has held the nation's biggest annual sports event, the Indianapolis 500-Mile Race, second is pretty lofty standing, particularly for an event in a town of 627 that probably not one Hoosier in a hundred could give directions to.

The Newport Hill Climb, says Carl Cook, now a veteran and aficionado, "snuck up on me."

Newport is north of Terre Haute near Indiana's western border. On the first weekend in October, it's a town of 100,000—more than a quarter-million visitors finding the little hamlet over the three days Friday through Sunday. "The numbers are astronomical," Carl said. "I don't know what the real number is, but it's in the hundreds of thousands." They come to watch cars speed up a hill. Real cars, some of them real old cars.

"I'd heard something about it," Carl said. "I happened to be driving by Newport on State Road 63 trying to get back to Terre Haute for some reason, and I kept passing Model A's. I'm thinking, 'What are all these old cars doing?'"

And then he noticed the billboards.

"Oh . . . it's Newport Hill Climb weekend."

Google it. Chances are it's the biggest Indiana event you've never heard of.

The first Indy 500 was in 1911. This event goes back farther, to the dawning of the automotive age when, it's surmised, owners of two of the first cars in the area raced each other up Newport's freak of geography: a 1,800-foot run up a 140-foot hill. Right through downtown. Starting point in the heart of town, straight in front of the courthouse. And it's still happening. Grandly.

"The Newport Hill Climb likely began as an 'innocent' challenge between two owners of 'new-fangled' automobiles," says literature from the event sponsor, the Newport Lions Club. "While early autos had trouble making it up to the crest of the hill, soon topping the 140-foot plus hilltop became common, but still a great struggle for the early gasoline engines. Then it wasn't just enough to top the hill; you had to be the fastest to climb it. The first Hill Climb was staged in 1909 and organized by the businessmen of Newport as a way to capitalize on the interest in climbing the hill." By 1916, the novelty was gone and the event died. But the hill stayed there, and the challenge. In the late 1960s, bringing it back with the spotlight on antique cars became a Newport Lions project. And—oh boy!—has it taken off.

The 2013 Hill Climb, the forty-fifth since the race resumed, drew more than 300 competing cars. The fastest car doesn't necessarily win. In each of 31 classes, rules say, "The time of each run is multiplied by the cubic inch displacement of the engine to determine the final score." In any given year, there will be about 330 hill-climbing cars, plus 500 show cars on display, acres and acres of vintage showpieces that are the highlight of much smaller shows across the country. Street rods and street machines are judged alongside classic antique vehicles in nine classes, with practice runs and opening ceremonies and, at 11:00 AM on Sunday, the first of the up-the-hill runs.

The three-day festival also includes "Big Wheel" races for kids three to eight, a pretty baby contest, a dog show, a gospel music jamboree, a queen contest, a cruise-in and street dance, a fireworks display, and a 20-hog pork barbecue.

Let Gayle Cook be your guide:

"Newport is a tiny town, with a courthouse [a candidate for Indiana's smallest county seat]. The main street that goes past the courthouse is out of town within two blocks. And then it goes straight up a hill.

"For 100 years or so, people have been testing their cars by going up the hill. Now it's very sophisticated, with timers and radio contact and loudspeakers. One at a time, cars start at the starting line and go up the hill and then out of sight.

Newport welcomes the world.

"And they go in classes: the Model T's, and the Model A's, and the Model A trucks, and the '30 cars, and the '40 cars, and the '50 cars.

"You are really racing against yourself. But, ohhh, there is a lot of calculation going on. They sit around talking—*'Then I let my clutch out'.. .'and then I . . .'*—they've got it all figured out, how to get the fast start. And sometimes they conk out and they have to go get vehicles to get them off the hill. And there are thousands and thousands of people there, and this tiny town becomes a giant flea market. Every house has something for sale in the front yard. It might be an antique shop, old clothes, a washing machine, crochet work. . . ."

It's the Newport Hill Climb, and it has Carl Cook hooked.

That one-day introduction on State Road 63 started it all. "It's 2008, we don't have the kids, and I said, 'Marcy, I'm going to take off for this car thing, if you don't mind.' I wound up taking my neighbor, Wayne Welken—he had no idea what it was, he grew up in Minnesota. So we got up on a Sunday morning, drove over there, and I was absolutely astounded. There are hundreds and hundreds of cars there, a car show, cars waiting to go up the hill, announcers, thousands of people who spent the whole day there—I came back and said, 'You will not believe what this thing is.'

"You look at this hill—that's a flat part of the state! What kind of hill could they have in Newport? It's a monster! It's a complete anomaly that that hill is there.

"So, I decided the next year, if I could, I was going to compete."

The Cooks already had their vintage cars. Two 1950 Studebakers. There's a story behind them.

George Ridgway recalls, "One Christmas I was thinking, 'What do you give a guy like Bill Cook?' Carl told me once the first car his parents had was a two-door 1950 Studebaker Champion, so I thought, 'How about a 1950 Champion?'

"Carl and I got on the Internet one day and found one on E-bay, up in Wisconsin. We bid it up and I think we got it for $4,500. We went up to pick it up, and cleaned it all up. It was in fair shape—on a scale of one to ten, I'd say it was a six. But it looked good. We set it all up to deliver it to Cedar Farm when we were all going to be there.

"Bill always likes devices, and I just got this new high-powered transit scope. I got Bill and Gayle outside, and we're looking at an eagle in a nest, all the way across the farm. I hear via earphones that the guy delivering the Studebaker is coming up the lane. I turned that transit right to the gate and told Bill, 'Look through here. What do you see?'

"He looked, and he said, 'I think I see a damned Studebaker!'

"Carl just became a fanatic about Studebakers. He asked his mother if she had anything about the first Studebaker they had. She looked in the basement and found the bill of sale from when they bought the car in 1957. Carl went from there to get the build order for the Christmas car—it and the one they bought were built thirty days apart, almost identical vehicles."

Not long afterward, Ridgway said he was driving down State Road 41 near Patoka, Indiana, and "saw this black 1950 Studebaker, four-door, sitting on the side of the road, for sale. I called the owner. If Bill's was a six on a scale of one-to-ten, this one was a nine. It really didn't need anything. I got it for $3,000."

He made the discovery and purchase one day after Carl's birthday. With Bill Cook taking Carl's place, the same plotters who pulled off the grand entry of Bill's Studebaker at Cedar Farm teamed to get Carl's gift car ready. One morning when Carl drove into his usual garage parking place, he saw a black 1950 Studebaker in his spot. "I knew it wasn't Dad's, because that was getting painted green," he said. "Then I got out and looked at it closer and saw it was a four-door, not two-door like Dad's. I was totally confused." And then the conspirators—Bill, George Ridgway, and Kevin Hazel (whose Silver Creek Engineering Co. was involved with the Cooks on some of their biggest projects)—stepped out from hiding places and yelled "Happy Birthday!"

There had been a bit of a clue. "The car had a bow around it," Carl said. And, it may have been a few days late, but "It was a *great* birthday."

Carl Cook actually took his Dad's light green, two-door 1950 Studebaker to Newport and entered it in the 2009 Hill Climb. "Mine was still being restored, so I took Dad's. I didn't get a very good time but I learned a lot.

"The next year, I was going to take mine. On the weekend of the Hill Climb, Dad and I were sitting at lunch Friday, and I told him I was going to stay up late to get the car ready because Sunday was the competition day. Dad said, 'It would be kind of fun to have mine in there again.' I told him, 'I can't drive two cars.' Ronan Young, one of the engineers, said, 'I'll take it.' Dad said, 'Sure, you take it, run it up the hill and let me know how you do.' I asked Dad, 'Do you want to go?' He said, 'I'm just not sure. I haven't been feeling all that great this week.'

"I had a feeling if he felt good he'd show up, and that's exactly what he did. He got up early Sunday morning and told Mom, 'Let's go to Newport.'

"She said, '*Where?*'

"They drove to Newport. Dad had never seen the place. I had been telling him about it, but unless you go you can't imagine what it is. He was blown away."

Among his surprises was finding among the Newport regulars a friend he normally saw in greatly different settings. Charles Webb, retired dean of IU's Jacobs School of Music and an eminent organist, brought his Cadillac limousine over for his son, Charlie, to drive it up the hill.

During the long wait for the run of his own Studebaker, "Dad took a nap in Charles Webb's Cadillac limousine," Carl said. "Then he sat along the side as we worked up the line. Ronan was still going to drive it up the hill—I entered it under his name. We got to the front row, about to be put in the starting position, and Dad said, 'Let's switch. *I'm* going to drive it up the hill.'

"They announced 'Ronan Young, from Spencer, Indiana,' but Dad was driving. I didn't have time to get it changed.

"And he *nailed* the start! I didn't know you could smoke the tires with a little Studebaker like that. But he did!

"And everybody at the starting line was, like, 'Wow!'

"He had a great time, 35.74 [seconds]—he beat my time by a full second. But he did run into shifting troubles on the hill. Going up a steep hill like that in a Studebaker it's hard to get it to go into what is called second overdrive. I've done it once—I got the black one to do it the first time I tried, and that year I got stuck in second.

"I got the records guy to change the entry, so Dad's name is in the record book now.

"I have gotten a better time every year I've gone. If I want a trophy I've got to get closer to 30. I've built a computer model with the car and I should be able to get under 30 seconds. But I'm a long way away. I'm still missing a few ingredients."

Carl and his black Studebaker were back in Newport in 2013, and they'll probably keep going for a while. But 2009 will stay his favorite Newport memory.

"When Dad drove that car up the hill, as far as I know it was the second-last time he drove that car before he died." Another time, when his paracentesis problems were starting to become severe, "I know he took it for a drive," Carl said. "He told me. I asked him how it went. He said, 'The car ran fine but my hands were cramping up. I had a tough time driving it home.' That's what would happen—he did it not too long after he'd been drained and he'd get hand cramps.

"He hadn't driven it for months before that time at Newport.

"He had a great time at the Hill Climb. And he loved watching all the old cars being driven as just regular cars, not museum pieces. You can walk around them, look at them, sit in them . . . It's much different than any antique car event."

If you go to Newport, go to the Hill Climb sometime, you'll find the Cook stamp is there in more than the record books.

"The weekend is the Newport Lions Club's big fund-raiser," Carl says. "Their lodge is right there on the main street across from the Courthouse. And their office building is an old 1890s bank building that had had some rather ill-advised modifications over the years. In 1968, the bank moved down the street and gave their building to the Lions. They got a Federal grant [under a program aimed at bringing doctors to small towns] and converted

Bill Cook at the starting line. "Nailed it!"

the building into a doctor's office with an apartment for the doctor to live upstairs." That didn't work, and the building they had left worked as a Hill Climb office but was low-glamour high-maintenance.

"When they converted it, they bricked in the windows, put a little drop ceiling in the interior, chopped it all up," Carl said. "And the roof was giving out. I remember at every climb—2008, 2009, 2010—there'd be periodic announcements about their rather desperate fund drive, 'We need $10,000 really bad to fix this roof.'

"Dad passed away and I got to thinking: He had a lot of fun with the Studebaker that day. I'm going to fix the roof.

On a new office wall, Hill Climb's past and present meet.

Facing. A little bit more than a "roof job" later, Newport's
Lions Club and the Hill Climb have a handsome home.

An early Hill Climb prize, more than a century later.

"It took me a while to get in touch with the right guy over there, but I finally did. I told him I wanted to come up and see the building, and I was going to donate the $10,000 for the roof.

"George Ridgway and I went over and looked. The roof was in bad shape. They repaired it as best they could but the underlying structure failed because of age. I told George, 'We may have to kick in a little more to fix it right—maybe $12,000.'

"I asked them if I could see the whole building, because normally you only see the front part of the first floor, the rest is closed off. They were scared to go up, because of the stairs. I looked at the whole building.

"I drove home that day and I got to thinking: 'You know what, why stop at the roof? We restore buildings. Let's just do the whole building.' I called George, he toured it with me, and he said, 'It's fixable. It would be a nice building.' I said, 'That's what we'll do.'

"I went back to the Lions, told them, and they were ecstatic. Structurally it was fine, except the roof. The heat had never been turned off. They had always done the best they could to repair it. The only problem we had was trying to figure out what it looked like before they turned it into a doctor's office. George made a sketch of what he thought an 1890s storefront would look like. There were pictures, but we could never really make out what the front looked like.

"But much to our amazement, when they pulled the brick façade off, the original storefront was still there. The windows were enormous—92 inches by 92, almost 8 feet square, the largest thermopane single-pane glass ever installed. That's what we put in. On the other side, we found some of the original interior wainscoting. A little section of the original floor survived; we used a pre-engineered floor but bought an identical pattern and color, so where the public walks now is on a floor that looks exactly like the original.

A celebration, a memory.

"The bank never remodeled. We could see the outline where the teller windows were. You could see the concrete pedestal for two walk-in vaults. We fixed up the whole office area. And of course it's computerized. The upstairs originally was a law office. The original woodwork was still there; we were able to salvage it. They used a common catalogue trim, which you can still order, so Joe Pritchett was able to get exact pieces to match up. The second-floor windows we were able to save. We were able put thermal pane in and get them to seal up."

And now the Newport Lions run their hill climb in style, including nice rest rooms on each floor. Time was that "primitive" was too high a compliment for the relief stations. Not now. The walls give witness to the building's past, including pictures that start with the first Hill Run in 1909. And there's a prayer a Newtown pastor, the Rev. Grover Williams, composed and read before the 1984 race:

Hill Climb Prayer

Here's to the lads and the cars they run,
   And the ladies that cheer them on,
And to Newport Hill that will remain
   Long after we all are gone.

Just give us a road and a wheel to turn,
   A song and some love and good will,
And rest and peace at the end of the race,
   When we reach the top of the hill.

—REV. GROVER WILLIAMS, 1984

There's one other thing.

"If you walk up to the building," Carl said, "on the right side of the front, right by the door, there was a bad brick patch—a good place to cover up with a plaque. They asked if I wanted to put something on it. I thought about it a while and decided we ought to do something.

"We put up a plaque." In true Bill Cook fashion, the plaque is simple and attractive.

Class H-1 means post-war cars, "orphan" make (designating cars whose manufacturer went out of production before 1970), six-cylinder, manual transmission. Studebaker's last cars were built in 1964.

Gayle was there to see all of that dedicated—she and Carl and Marcy and Eleanor and Shaunacee, Eleanor's big sister who had joined the family by then. "We finished the building in the spring," Carl said, "and they had a ribbon-cutting."

"That plaque," Gayle Cook says, "is, I think, an excellent little memorial."

Shaunacee was 11 when she joined the family. Through her own church youth work, Marcy had known Shaunacee for years, and Carl recalls her telling him once, "Shaunacee is amazing. That would be the kind of child I would like to adopt." On May 1, 2012, they officially became a family of four. "I'm sorry Dad never got to meet her or she got to meet him," Carl said.

Eleanor has a special day ahead. "I have a copy of *Ready, Fire, Aim!* in which Dad wrote a little note to her," Carl said. "We've got the book put away so she won't tear it to pieces, but I got it out and read the note. He wrote a fairly long paragraph and I could tell, and rightly so because of her age and his age, that he wrote it knowing full well that by the time she could read it he wouldn't be there. It's kind of a touching paragraph. I won't even paraphrase it." Some day.

PART FOUR

Looking toward the Future

Bill Cook's office, intact. Building visitors call it "the highlight of the tour."

Fourteen

2013
Was Golden

191

"A lot of people say it's comfortable to see the office still there, to see the light on. Tour groups tell us that's the highlight of the tour."

—*Carl Cook*

*I*t was Dotter Institute director Fred Keller who said at the June 1, 2011, Celebration of Life for Bill Cook that he knew from conversations, "He was proud to pass Carl the baton." Normalcy wasn't part of the deal—at least not for a while. "The whole month of June was busy," Carl Cook said, once he'd had time to reflect. "We had a vacation with Marcy's family, and we had a trip to Germany. I remember being so relieved when we got back from Germany—I didn't have to go anywhere and I didn't have anything hanging over my head. I felt, 'I'm just not going to do anything for a while.'"

But a profound change of life was coming, had arrived, really. Carl allowed himself that brief catch-your-breath break, then, like the company itself, he moved along. Comfortably.

Among the ways Bill Cook had planned for those days that came to pass in April 2011 was to take the legal steps that made the transition of power within the company seamless. Years before it had been established in legal documents that Carl Cook would be his father's successor on the corporate board. Death came on Friday afternoon; work resumed on schedule on Monday morning, with no in-house announcements necessary, no awkwardness: a model of continuity.

In his last years, Carl says, "Dad had kind of maneuvered himself into a position where he didn't have to do anything for anybody. He could just choose what he wanted to do, and so, as a result, there really wasn't anything that had to change.

"That's really why the transition was so smooth. It wasn't like he had his fingers in every conceivable change. There were projects and things where he had to make decisions, but it didn't change the way the company ran at all. If there was something major going on that we needed to get his take on, we talked about it. He and I talked virtually every day, when both of us were in the office—if we were both here, we talked."

And later? Since?

"Oh, it's lonelier. It is lonelier.

"Is it different? Not really. But he isn't there."

Kem Hawkins, whose Cook Group presidency didn't change, looks at the same transitional period from an obviously different view, but winds up with the same word.

He smiles as he remembers when he—a career high school band director whom Bill Cook first noticed when Carl was a marching saxophonist under him—capped a 20-year rise by becoming president of Cook Group. "Bill was pretty heavily involved in my first year as president; the second year, strikingly less. From that point on it was just an incredible relationship.

"He would come in here . . . if I had a new product on my desk he'd light up, even at the end. Bill could forget all the things that were bothering him physically, if you had a new product to show him. His eyes would light up. He was high. And as soon as he walked out, he was hurting. But for those moments, he still had that twinkle."

And now, the difference without him? "The only thing I can say is he is profoundly missed. He wasn't a boss. There was a relationship, and the relationship was not just friendship, there was some father in it, mentor, sage—it runs the whole gamut.

"Probably the overwhelming feeling is lonely."

"THE HIGHLIGHT OF THE TOUR"

The second-floor windows looking out over the welcoming outdoor fountain still include the ones for Bill Cook's office, where the look inside those windows hasn't changed a bit these recent days, months, and years without its only ever occupant. The office is long, so much so its 42-foot length makes its 20-foot width seem narrow. His desk and computer sit almost in the middle between flanking walls that look meticulously planned to give prominence

to galleries of photos and plaques or framed certification of honorary degrees, awards, or other recognitions. And no one but overnight custodians ever sees it dark. "Every morning, one of the first things I do is walk over and turn on his office light—it makes me feel better," says Kem Hawkins, whose office is next door.

Carl Cook operates in another wing of the building. Whatever thoughts he might have given to moving into the other area—maybe even *the* room—must have been short-lived. "For right now, I can't move myself there, or change anything in there. At the time I said I was going to leave things as they were for at least a year. I still don't feel like trying to do anything there.

"A lot of people say it's comfortable to see the office still there, to see the light on. Tour groups tell us that's the highlight of the tour."

Bill Cook's desk stands as it was, including a jar for the "Ashes of Problem Employees."

Treasured awards and pictures fill Bill Cook's office walls.
"He picked every one of them himself."

The straight-on view from Bill Cook's chair.

The walls are filled with Bill's favorite photographs, mementos, and framed treasures, his own island in the middle of the vastness was fully equipped and comfortable—the office "home" he wanted. "The thing I like about them is he picked every one of them himself," Aimee Hawkins-Mungle said. "And in just about every one of them, he's smiling."

SPANNING THE GLOBE

In 2013, the business empire that Bill Cook started with his bare hands celebrated its fiftieth anniversary. Truly it was golden. It took the company until its forty-third year to have its first $1-billion sales year (2006). It took just seven more years—to that fiftieth year—for sales for the first time to pass $2 billion (2013).

The biggest international Golden Anniversary celebration, bringing in European and North American sales representatives and management, was in late July in Las Vegas, but that was just one gala event of sixteen that took place around the globe from April in Ireland through November in Australia. The Las Vegas event and a more local observance involving Blooming-

Preserved, too, was what Bill Cook frequently called "the world's ugliest trophy," which the professional basketball team he owned in Manchester, England, won in the national championship.

In a special spot on his office wall is the award Bill Cook called "probably the highlight of my business career" when the Society for Interventional Radiology made him the first non-physician to receive its Gold Medal. "That didn't come from my peers, it came from people we served," he said.

ton-area employees at IU's Assembly Hall and Cook Hall in early-August brought out the most prominent Bloomington headquarters representatives, but top officials opened their schedules to be sure that there was some core representation at every one of the events. Each included tributes to the company's late founder and references to keeping alive his dream that built the company from such tiny beginnings to such gigantic adulthood as a business enterprise.

In Bloomington, certainly, and perhaps in much of America, the whole Bill Cook story—the start from a $1,500 shoestring, the growth, all that went into what the man meant to the "culture" of the company—is familiar, but what about, say, China?

"Ooooh, yes, particularly the young people," says Cook Medical president Pete Yonkman. "They [young Cook leaders in China] didn't know Bill personally. But I think they really, really get the culture of Cook. They love the stories—not the facts and figures but the people involved, how he built this business." China, Japan, Ireland, India, and Australia all were fiftieth-anniversary stop-in points for Yonkman—who wasn't alone in thinking that, as exciting and significant as the Golden Anniversary galas were, how very much better the celebration would have been with the founder around to enjoy them. "I thought about that a lot," Yonkman said. "He'd have loved it."

The facts and figures involved in Bill Cook's company's first 50 years aren't a bad story, themselves. The Cook climb, measured in sales, was astonishing: from an $18,000 first year in 1964, to the first million-dollar sales year in the company's seventh year in business, 1970; to the first $10-million year in 1976; the first $100-million in 1983; the first half-billion-dollar year, 2001; all the way to those two latest landmarks in 2006 and 2013. It has grown geographically as well, since that apartment bedroom beginning, as the sixteen gala locations across the globe showed. The most accelerated expansion of sales in recent years has come in the newest region to be part of the Cook empire, the grouping known as Australasia, encompassing Australia, New Zealand, China, Japan, Taiwan, and Indonesia.

"Five years ago that represented 11 percent of our business," Kem Hawkins said. "Today I think it's 25 percent of our business. In another five years, it's very likely to be the size of what we do in the United States. Asia is just exploding. I think we did over $500 million this year. I see that growing to a billion in five years."

The net effect has been a total increase in sales, despite a general fall-off in the U.S. economy in 2008 and a slow recovery. The big bank failures and turbulent economy of course had an impact on Cook as well as every other business. "In October of 2008, it was like someone dropped a sledgehammer," Hawkins says. "It was the first time I ever witnessed an impact of an economic downturn on the medical side of business. We went from smokin' [sales-increase percentages] in double digits to 5.4 percent. But never negative.

"During that time, in the rest of '08 and '09, when everybody else was laying off, we pushed it hard." Being a family-owned corporation, with no stockholders clamoring for higher profit margins, once again provided the managerial freedom that Bill Cook always valued. Still, there were comparisons available with all competitors. "We compare ourselves to the public companies—we get all their reports," Hawkins said. "When we look back over the last 10 years, we've been one and two in growth with all of our competitors."

Greater entry into the worldwide market helped stabilize things. Cook's ratio of foreign sales to domestic "has climbed a little bit," Carl Cook says. "I'm sure in 2006 it was probably 60/40, U.S. This year it will probably drop below 50 percent because China and Japan, even Europe, still seem to be climbing faster than the U.S."

AN INDY-TO-FRENCH LICK TRAIN?

There's still a Bill Cook touch to the guiding philosophies of the company, of course, but it goes even a little deeper than that, Pete Yonkman feels.

As much as anyone in the Cook hierarchy, young lawyer Yonkman studied Bill Cook, looked and listened hard for what was unique in the man, for what there was to be learned from observation. The thoughts that began to run through his mind that April day when Bill died still do, months and years later. Leadership is a hollow word for what burned deepest among Yonkman's memories of Bill Cook's style. Watching him put an idea to work, Yonkman said, "You understand that once you have a vision of something—it could be grand or small—the *relentlessness* with which you have to go after it, to get other human beings to go with you on the ride. He was an unbelievable master at that. Everybody wanted to come along. I don't know exactly what it was. You knew it was going to be interesting, and you were going to be doing things you've never done before. He was always searching for something new and something different and something hard that was going to be worthwhile.

Pete Yonkman, Gayle Cook, Steve Ferguson, Carl Cook,
and Kem Hawkins at Cook company's 50th-anniversary celebration.

No. 50 a time for hoopla for Cook Group president Kem Hawkins.

Tom Osborne, from first employee at 18 to vice president, speaks with a giant backdrop of a happy moment with the man who called him "a genius"—Bill Cook.

"Red-neck" comedian Jeff Foxworthy entertains.

Carl Cook

Honored employee Janet (Sue) Watkins being congratulated by
Kem Hawkins, Steve Ferguson, Pete Yonkman, and John Kamstra.

The night's applause, for Gayle and Carl Cook.

"I was only around him for ten years. The first part of that, he was much more engaged in the business. You saw the fieriness, the entrepreneur. You were watching the evolution of a person who has done about all he could do in business and is starting to think of the world in a bigger way—in terms of philanthropy, and trying to set the world up for other people—not just in the business but even the community: trying to make the community a better place, for no other reason that he *could,* and it was the *right* thing to do.

"The big issues of the company he still was very interested in. The day-to-day sales numbers, he really didn't care about.

"He was always very self-aware. He understood his relationship to other people, in terms of power structures—he was very, very cognizant of that, and extremely good at it. I think people often misconstrued what he was—it was a conscious choice he made, to be the guy from Bloomington, not the sophisticated businessman from Boston. He could have been. He chose not to. So, sometimes people mistook that for a smallness, a 'rube.'" Laughter interrupted his musing. "One thing he never was, was a rube.

"He knew he was dying. He talked about it. He knew his last few years. He would work out in the morning, then he would come into my office for 45 minutes to an hour . . . just talk. When he started the [heart fluid] draining, I think that's when he figured out he was dying. He talked a lot about the process of dying, the moment of dying."

But he also talked of other things, including a project that never came to public light: setting up a railroad connection between Indianapolis and French Lick. "He wanted to run actual trains Indianapolis to French Lick—self-propelled commuter trains, which only one company in the country built. You could put about 100 people on them—cost about $5 million, there were existing tracks. The day we were going to sign the contract, the company went bankrupt. We were that close.

"It was a great example to me of how he operated, his vision. So many people in Indiana say, 'Let's build mass transit to Indianapolis.' He was, 'Let's stop talking, put trains on the rails, and see if anybody rides them.' He wanted to see if mass transit actually worked.

"He had an awareness of his power, his sense of what his power was. He never abused it. He used the good side of it: Can you make things any better? Can you change the way this dynamic works? Can you actually influence the way people think about mass transit?

"People sometimes mistook him for how simple he spoke, how simple he dressed—how casual he was, the way he interacted with people. He had a real sense of how to use words, how words had an impact on people. It was never dull, never without making a point, nothing extraneous—all very simple. That's kind of the way all of his dealings were—right to the point, and he understood how to get to the point very fast. He could get you off-kilter by being so blunt. But that was intentional. He was always trying to get people away from their defenses, to the real thing."

It's all part of what Pete Yonkman hears when he hears "Bill Cook" and "culture" and thinks of the company's future, even as it runs today. "I don't think there's a conscious 'what would Bill think, or what would Bill do?' But . . . sometimes a two- or three-year employee, a product manager, will have this great presentation, and it says nothing—a lot of fluff. There's a lot of value in the numbers and the assumptions, but . . . 'Where's the thing in this that's going to make a difference? Stop the fluff and give me the meat of it.' After being around Bill, you just *can't* not think that way."

"THIS PLACE IS MAGICAL"

A few years into operation, Old Centrum is living the life Bill Cook saw for it: as not just a grand old building but a self-sustaining hub of Indiana Landmarks' preservation operations. "That was such an important part of his vision—he believed this could work for us, and it really has," Marsh Davis said two years after the building's dedication.

"We're not at the point where the operation is bringing in lots of money, but it's hard to break even, and we're doing better than that. The program is entirely new, without sophisticated marketing, a track record—this is a whole new world for us, and it has been really good.

"We can have several hundred people here—for a lecture in Grand Hall we've had 600 people. We have weddings—that's why Bill was so focused on catering facilities and really all the details involved there. We do arts events, including concerts and gallery shows, and we also do corporate events. A Pulitzer Prize-winning composer, Joseph Schwantzer, did a world premier here, and afterward he said, 'What *is* this? This place is magical!'

"I got an e-mail from one of the local foundations that wants to have an event here and he said they were 'enchanted' by the place. This venue is unique, and I mean that in the truest sense of the word. I love to show this

The makeover begins on a building that "was really crummy at the time."

building to people. When I take them into the Grand Hall for the first time, almost inevitably they say, 'Wow!'

A significant part of the Cooks' renovation involved bringing back to full richness, clarity, and power the building's organ. "Charles Webb [a renowned organist as well as former dean of IU's celebrated Jacobs School of Music] helped in a big way there," Marsh Davis said. "The acoustics were always very good, but I think we have improved them. We put carpeting in the aisles but not under the pews to give it a more resonant sound. We also added a lot of oak flanking the organ. Originally there was a multi-tiered pulpit area. We had to make one flat stage. So we had to add a lot of oak.

"What used to be a nasty church basement Bill had a vision for right away: 'Let's beautify this space and make it rentable.' It works very well now as an art gallery, so we have art shows down there on a regular basis.

"He saw that we could make this work for us financially. The 2012 calendar year we had 33 weddings, 244 events—120 non-profit events, 77 performance/art gallery shows, and 14 corporate events—with an estimated 38,000 people, and a modest net profit. We anticipate it will grow.

"When we took this on, one thing we really stressed was we were not going to take our eye off the ball, off what we do as a preservation organization. This was going to enhance that. Many of those 38,000 people who came through here in 2012 had no association with preservation, but they were exposed to it here, in an inspiring, historical place.

"It also has connected us with people of influence in the community who come in here, see what we've done, and realize we mean what we say when we talk about sustaining the life of this community. This was a blight in this neighborhood. We took something that was falling apart and revitalized this corner of the neighborhood. It has also opened some doors in the philanthropic world. Senator Lugar has been a great champion in this."

One of Bill Cook's last public outreaches had been an Op-Ed column he put together, which ran in several newspapers—including his hometown Bloomington *Herald-Times* and his "other" hometown paper, the Canton *Ledger*. It centered on the very point Davis was making, about Old Centrum's utility, beyond its recovered beauty, and in the man's own words it laid out Bill Cook's idea of yesterday's relevance today.

> Why historic preservation?
> Because it helps communities.
>
> As I stood on the stage in the wonderful old Central Avenue Methodist Church in Indianapolis' Old Northside historic district, announcing the support my family is giving to assist in restoring and converting it to the Indiana Landmarks Center, I was fully prepared for the inevitable question:
> Why?
> My wife Gayle and son Carl and I have been asked this question more than a few times about our historic renovation projects. And

while our objectives may vary from place to place, the big-picture reason is the same each time:

Restoring historic structures helps communities.

I got involved in restoration projects more than 30 years ago when a serious cardiac illness sidelined me from my medical device business. When it looked as though I might never be able to work in an office again, Gayle and I thought renovating historic buildings would be a good idea. It would allow us to contribute to society and make money. Fortunately, in time my health improved and I was able to return to my executive role. But we stuck with preservation, even as we grew our medical device business. Why? Because we love historic buildings' character, history and beauty, but also because we've seen the impact preservation projects can have on people's daily lives. We've witnessed it in Bloomington, where revitalizing historic buildings around the courthouse square helped transform a faded downtown into a popular commercial and retail center. We've seen it in French Lick and West Baden, once struggling communities now thriving as travel destinations.

In these and other places, there's a snowball effect that follows a restoration project. One restored building leads to others, and, pretty soon, you have a thriving area where there was once lack of investment and neglect.

In other words, saving landmarks that reconnect us to heritage also spurs economic development and community revitalization. That's why such luminaries of Indiana business as Eli Lilly, Herman Krannert, and James Hoover founded Indiana Landmarks 50 years ago—not simply because they personally liked vintage places, but because they saw the economic and community value in historic buildings.

Admittedly, when you're looking at a tired old building, the opportunities it presents are not always obvious. For example, when the West Baden Springs Hotel was collapsing, experts suggested that Indiana Landmarks "call it a ruin and let people crawl on it." Fortunately for the people of Orange County and all Hoosiers, Indiana Landmarks didn't listen to that advice.

Which leads me back to the question I hear so often:
Why?

> Simply put, we believe in the communitywide impact of historic preserva-
> tion. It's not just about old buildings, and it's not simply about preserving
> the past. It's about building for the future, and benefiting entire communities.

"He saw that we could make this work for us financially," Marsh Davis said.
Of course he did. Unless he had, chances are the Cooks' preservation effort
would have been focused somewhere else.

COOK BUILDINGS ON THREE CAMPUSES

Within a few months after Bill Cook's death, Rose-Hulman Institute of Technology at Terre Haute, Indiana, announced establishment of the William
Alfred Cook Laboratory for Bioscience Research. In 2013, as a highlighted
feature of the sixtieth anniversary reunion of Bill Cook's graduation class of
1953, Northwestern University rededicated its Cook Hall, a 21-year-old, six-
story structure formerly known as the Materials & Life Sciences Building.
The Cook name is also on the football stadium at Rose-Hulman, the basketball practice facility-museum at Indiana University, and the music library for
IU's Jacobs School of Music.

Carl Cook presented the $500,000 gift to Rose-Hulman that established
the laboratory there. "My father was a cross-disciplinary inventor who used
engineering technology to solve complex problems in the field of internal
medicine," said Carl, a Rose-Hulman trustee. "Our family is proud to help
advance this cross-disciplinary approach to learning and experimentation."

A Rose-Hulman announcement said the new laboratory "allows students
to develop their knowledge of the biological sciences through the study of
plant life and organisms." Rose-Hulman president Matt Branam said the
1,350-square foot facility "will serve as a living laboratory for our students
[and] will greatly enhance our campus appearance, showcase our commitment to the life sciences, and help us produce Rose-Hulman graduates who
can combine superior problem-solving abilities with an awareness of the role
of biology and botany in technical solutions."

Gayle Cook and Steve and Connie Ferguson attended the re-dedication at
Northwestern, which included participation by NU president Morton Scha-
piro and a video tribute to Bill that ran in the building lobby during the day
amid science displays. "There's a cluster of science buildings at Northwestern," Gayle said. "Because now so many sciences are related because of computers and need to work together, they have connected all the science buildings with pass-throughs, so you can walk from one building to another—and

The Medical Field Service School

United States Army

This is to certify that

WILLIAM A. COOK, PRIVATE, RA16 369 440

has satisfactorily completed the

MEDICAL INTERMEDIATE COURSE (OPERATING ROOM TECHNICIAN - MOS 1861)
CONDUCTED AT
MEDICAL FIELD SERVICE SCHOOL AND BROOKE ARMY HOSPITAL

Given at Brooke Army Medical Center, Fort Sam Houston, Texas this 26th day of March 19 54

M. E. GRIFFIN, Major General, MC
Commanding

Lt Colonel, MSC,
Secretary

Bill's certificate of graduation from the Army's Medical Field Service School at Fort Sam Houston, where he was an operating room technician. He also did some teaching. He entered the Army months after graduation from Northwestern.

it *is* warmer in the winter, on Lake Michigan. We toured these labs, which have equipment you can't fathom." Molecular biosciences, biophysics, neurobiology, physiology and biophysics are the departments in Cook Hall.

The educational gifts honor a man who once had his own thoughts of going through medical school and having a career as a doctor. What most people don't know, Gayle Cook says with a smile, "is he actually was accepted by a medical school—Washington University of St. Louis." That came after he had completed two years in the army, including time at Fort Sam Houston in Texas as an operating-room technician and—after taking some courses in physics and organic chemistry at Trinity University—an instructor for doctors and nurses in the physics of anesthetics. He came out of the Army in May 1955, spent a year getting introduced to working in private business, and in late-summer 1956, Gayle says, "He went to St. Louis, went to the registration office, and said, 'When do I need to withdraw so somebody else can have my place?' They said, 'Today.' So he wrote a letter of withdrawal right there."

Why?

"I don't think he wanted to study seven more years."

THE LIST GOES ON

Meanwhile, for Carl Cook, family and future move along, intertwined at the office and in the special Cook area of philanthropy and preservation, with a sprinkling in there of just plain fun.

Above and facing. Metamorphosis in Solsberry: Yoho's store is reborn. *Photos by Larry Shute, CFC.*

Just as in the Bill-and-Gayle heydays, there are the little projects as well as the big, as the new era carries on a tradition of nostalgic revivals, e.g., the charm of the Laconia General Store, which was brought back (including its separate Democrat and Republican Liars' Benches out front) as a complement to Cedar Farm, just a few miles away. Yoho's General Store is in downtown Solsberry, which is Laconia with a little more ice cream. Solsberry, unincorporated and population-unlisted, is in Greene County just west of Bloomington at the near midpoint between Newark and Cincinnati, the Indiana versions, down the road from Rosie's Diner (with its sign out front: "You've got to be tough to eat here") and from the Second-Longest Railroad Trestle in the world, its length traversable (though not legally) in a vertiginous hour and a half on foot (it's also quite high). And, in October, when the leaves change, Solsberry and its trestle are smack in the middle of heaven.

Jim Murphy is from Greene County. "I went to Solsberry as a kid—I absolutely remember going in to Yoho's, getting ice cream." Marcy Cook, an IU Kelley School of Business graduate and a tax accountant before her marriage to Carl, is an entrepreneur herself in her revived home area. She opened an Indiana-stocked craft shop, Ellie Mae's Boutique, honoring her grandmother's name, next to Yoho's, a two-generation family store that at the time seemed in its last days. Bill Cook was there for Marcy's grand opening, and that's the reason for the Cook-Yoho's tie. "Mr. Cook wanted us to buy and get the Yoho store going again, because it has always been a dynamic part of the town," Murphy said. Acquisition by CFC kept the store from closing, and after months of renovation, the spruced-up Yoho's reopened December 1, 2012, with a new foundation, new floors, wiring, plumbing, counters, cases, sidewalks, and ramps that made it handicap-accessible.

Two dates in particular heralded its return.

In its seventh week, the area was raked by a near-tornado—torrential rain and 70-mph straight-line winds that damaged several homes and left hundreds without electricity. And then it got cold. Next day, Jim Murphy drove over from Bloomington "to see if the store had been damaged. The parking lot was full when I got there. Cars were everywhere—on a Wednesday morning! I wondered, 'What in the world is going on?'" The renovation had included a back-up generator. Yoho's had the only power in the area "so many of the locals had gathered for warmth, lights, and food," Murphy found, "in a sheltered environment, surrounded by friends. It was great!"

And then, on July 4, 2013, the area's biggest fireworks show drew a crowd that kept Yoho's ice cream cone line unending for most of the afternoon and evening.

"The store is doing pretty good business," Carl said. "We've got the Tivoli Theater going now [another preservation/renovation of a generations-old movie house in downtown Spencer, a county away from Yoho's, to the north].

"We've just bought a farm that has a classic old barn—it's touch-and-go but savable. The Pritchetts just started working on it. And it has a 1830s farmhouse in pretty good shape—eventually we'll want to restore that, too. It's called Yellow Rose Ranch—a hundred acres." There will be more of those preservations and restorations. That's a list that might never end, because for all whom the man touched, for all he inspired, the Bill Cook culture didn't end with his death. Throughout these pages, from Beck's Mill through Old Centrum, we have met people who retain permanent memories of what they saw that made Bill Cook different—different from anyone, everyone:

> Preservationist Tina Connor was captivated by the way Bill Cook saw old buildings: *"He was a problem-solver, he liked fixing things, to make them work in the twenty-first century . . . he loved these old things but he also dearly loved figuring out where to put the elevator and how to make it work right—things it didn't originally have but needed today."*

> Architect George Ridgway recalls the first look inside 199-year-old Beck's Mill: *"Of course it was in terrible shape, and Bill right away was telling me everything he wanted to do, just like he did with every other project: 'I want to fix this, fix that, take that wheel off . . .' His first time inside the place!"*

In "a crumbling old building," Old Centrum church, Indiana Landmarks director Marsh Davis said, *"What used to be a nasty church basement Bill had a vision for right away: 'Let's beautify this space and make it rentable.' It works very well now as an art gallery, so we have art shows down there on a regular basis."*

Steve Ferguson, perhaps his closest friend, walked streets around the world with him and found it *"astounding the detail he could see. And the observations about people."*

Pete Yonkman saw Bill in his last years *"starting to think of the world in a bigger way—in terms of philanthropy, and trying to set the world up for other people—not just in the business but even the community: trying to make the community a better place, for no other reason than he could, and it was the right thing to do."*

In a wide range of areas and circumstances, people who knew him best saw in his many and seemingly disparate interests—with buildings, people, towns and downtowns—a consistency to Bill Cook. He was a type, a noun that maybe never has been used on anyone before—beyond a visionary, a *re*-visionary. He saw ways not just to bring back or extend life but to revive and renew it—not just to wake Rip Van Winkle up but to put him in today's clothes, make him computer-savvy—and let him *live!*

This was a man who almost certainly knew he was dying but, unlike the rest of us who might have withdrawn into morose seclusion, used every one of his last hours, right to the end, to create, to give beauty and function to the world he was leaving.

In his last days, his homestretch, all around him knew he was in a hurry. Obviously so did he. But he envisioned and carried out creations and re-creations those last four years, scornful of death, working wonders he knew he might never see and certainly would not have the chance to savor as often as he would have liked.

Oh, he was a master of savoring. The times were countless when he came up with excuses to make the drive, one more time, down the country roads and up the lanes that laid before his eyes the masterpieces at West Baden and French Lick, fully entitled to feel almost God-like responsibility for those breathtaking sights.

These were not four years spent winding down a life but completing a legacy. These were four years of robust activity punctuated by stops at the hospital for the painful and exhausting paracentesis that disturbed but did not break the rhythm of his creative and re-creative life.

Bill Cook: Re-Visionary. A word of his own.

Postscript

The grandeur of Bill Cook's contributions that will last long beyond his lifetime expanded months after his death, thanks to a long-time colleague's respect and generosity. Gunar Gruenke, president of the Conrad Schmitt Studios organization, which was a partner with Bill and Gayle Cook at West Baden, French Lick, and so many of their greatest restoration projects, made a trip to Bloomington to visit Cook's crypt at his self-chosen mausoleum, Valhalla Memory Garden. The result of that visit is a stunningly beautiful stained glass work that glorifies not just the building but appropriately reflects onto the Cook crypt.

The suburban-Milwaukee firm said in a statement that Gruenke on his visit "saw that there was no stained glass in the transepts of the large cruciform mausoleum. Feeling that this was not right for someone who had dedicated so much of his life to supporting art and architecture, Gunar recognized an opportunity to honor Bill and his work by beautifying his final resting place."

It was done in a way both personal and precedent-setting. First came selection of a design. Inspiration for it came, the company said, from "Bill's appreciation for art and beauty" and "the generous spirit of the Cook family." CSS's creative team consulted with Gayle and Carl Cook about an appropriate theme for the dominant stained-glass window, while considering, too, what the company called a "practical concern: an installation that would allow ample light to penetrate the space." After exploration of a variety of subjects that included sketches and images of saints and the four Evangelists, the creative team's choice was "non-denominational—choirs of angels that transcend religious boundaries."

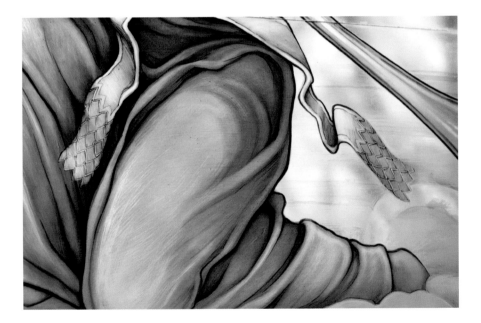

Artistry soft and spectacular bathes the Bill Cook crypt with constant warmth and late-afternoon glory since its installation at Valhalla Memory Gardens. This original work, commissioned by Gunar Gruenke, includes a personal link—a caduceus medical insignia in an angel's headdress and stylized representations of the Z design of the Cook company's "Triple-A" stent on her sash.

When consideration turned to a choice of materials and techniques, things became nouveau. The company's project director, Kevin Grabowski, collaborated with CSS artists to create an original piece for the Cook project, using what the company described "an innovative technique" which Grabowski had seen at a workshop. "The design was painted with brilliantly colored enamels onto single panes of glass, which were then fused to safety glass with a silicon-based laminate."

The technique was new but the design traditional. "The choirs of angels float on translucent clouds that allow the colors beyond the window to show through," the CSS statement says. "The scene obscures the line between inside and outside, so that the doors to the mausoleum become less of a barrier. This effect is amplified due to the absence of the lead lines characteristic in traditional leaded stained glass. The final installation allows ample amounts of natural light to enter the room while enhancing the spiritual atmosphere of the solemn space."

Installation came in the summer of 2013, when Cook Group internationally was celebrating the 50th anniversary of the company's founding by Bill and Gayle in a spare bedroom at their eastside Bloomington apartment.

One of the Cooks' fascinations with the Conrad Schmitt company's work was their artists' almost puckish penchant for working something unique and personal—not about them but their patrons of the moment. And it's there in the window. An angel's headdress includes the caduceus medical insignia, and on her sash are stylized representations of the Z design of the company's groundbreaking "Triple-A" stent.

And it all came with a bonus, even for the artists. "After installation," the company announcement said, "the design team noticed an unanticipated effect: the figures in the glass reflect on the polished stone walls, repeating the pattern again and again. The whole space dances with angels, a fitting tribute to a benevolent and compassionate man."

Both Gayle Cook and Gruenke noted that theirs was a partnership with a long history. The company Bill founded, Gruenke said, was "at the forefront of medical device technology. His success in the medical field allowed him to follow his heart and procured the preservation of some of Indiana's most notable historic buildings, including West Baden Springs Hotel and the French Lick Springs Resort and Casino in southern Indiana. Conrad Schmitt Studios assisted the Cook team with the interior restoration at these locations, as well as at a number of others, including Monroe County Courthouse in Bloomington, Indiana Landmarks Center in Indianapolis, the Benedictine Monastery at Ferdinand, and the Tivoli Theatre in Spencer." The partnership "has helped bring the Cooks' passion for artistry to many of their state's most important cultural institutions [and] revived the economic growth and cultural appreciation of many cities and towns across Indiana," Gruenke said. And the partnership continues: Gayle and Carl Cook joined with Conrad Schmitt in 2014 in restoring a large stained glass dome at Indiana State University in Terre Haute.

Index

BOB HAMMEL'S career choice was journalism: sports writing his specialty. He practiced it in a number of different Indiana towns, starting in his native Huntington as a sports editor at 17. A few days after turning 30, at the highest professional level he had attained—as tenth man on an outstanding ten man sports staff at *The Indianapolis News*—he chose to do what most would consider a step-down. He left Indianapolis to be sports editor of the Bloomington *Herald-Telephone*, heading a two man staff.

The editor-publisher who brought him in, Perry Stewart, was as much a visionary as Bill Cook. Stewart promised something more than the usual small-town paper's sports coverage, and, though he died just four years later at 41 after long-time problems with diabetes, his successors in management carried out his wishes by financing Hammel's coverage of what ultimately added up to 23 NCAA basketball Final Fours, dozens of other championship events in a variety of sports, and, unprecedented for so small an American newspaper, 5 Olympic Games. Those years included Hammel's writing what now totals 13 books, his induction into 5 Halls of Fame, presidencies of 3 national sportswriters' organizations, and selection 17 times as Indiana Sportswriter of the Year.

For 40 years, Hammel and Bill Cook shared the same town without much more than crossing paths. That changed in the fall of 2006 when Cook at 75 agreed to cooperate with the first biography of him. Hammel was by then retired after 52 years in journalism and was 70 himself. That biography, *The Bill Cook Story: Ready, Fire, Aim!,* was published in 2008 by Indiana University Press. This is Act II of their joint tale.

EDITORIAL DIRECTOR · *Bob Sloan*

MARKETING DIRECTOR · *Dave Hulsey*

PRODUCTION DIRECTOR · *Bernadette Zoss*

PROJECT MANAGER · *Michelle Sybert*

INTERIOR DESIGN/COMPOSITION · *Pamela Rude*

JACKET DESIGN · *Mike Galimore and Pamela Rude*